**Evaluating Community
Treatment Programs**

Evaluating Community Treatment Programs

Tools, Techniques,
and a Case Study

Edited by

Mercedese M. Miller
Social, Educational Research
and Development, Inc.

Lexington Books
D.C. Heath and Company
Lexington, Massachusetts
Toronto London

Library of Congress Cataloging in Publication Data

Main entry under title:

Evaluating community treatment programs.

   Bibliography: p.
   Includes index.
   1. Community-based corrections. 2. Halfway houses. 3. Rehabilitation of criminals. I. Miller, Mercedese M.
HV8665.E93   365'.3   74-33597
ISBN 0-669-99101-5

Copyright © 1975 by D.C. Heath and Company.

All rights reserved. No part of this publication may be reproduced or transmitted in any form or by any means, electronic or mechanical, including photocopy, recording, or any information storage or retrieval system, without permission in writing from the publisher.

Published simultaneously in Canada.

Printed in the United States of America.

International Standard Book Number: 0-669-99101-5

Library of Congress Catalog Card Number: 74-33597

Contents

	List of Figures	ix
	List of Tables	xi
	Preface	xiii
Chapter 1	**Introduction**	1
	Purposes of This Study	1
	Community Correctional Centers	1
	The Role and Purposes of Evaluation	2
	SERD/CHHDC: A Community Treatment Center for Youthful Offenders	3
	How to Use This Study	9
Chapter 2	**Designing and Using Evaluation Systems and Techniques**	11
	The General Setting	11
	Kinds and Levels of Evaluation	12
	Selecting an Outside Evaluator	15
	Cost of Evaluation	16
	Methods and Techniques in Conducting Evaluations	17
	Expectations of Evaluations	19
	Issues in the Evaluation of Community Correctional Centers	21
Chapter 3	**Forms and Procedures**	23
	Introduction	23
	Written Procedures Manuals	23
	Intake Procedures	25
	Intake Form Codes	30
	Family Information Form Codes	34

	Program Plan	37
	Parole Procedures and Forms	38
	Follow-up	38

Chapter 4	**The Management Information System (MIS)**	51
	Introduction	51
	Goals and Objectives	51
	The MIS Report Form	52
	MIS Summary Forms	62

Chapter 5	**A Case Study Evaluation: The SERD/Congress Heights Human Development Center (SERD/CHHDC), 1971-1973**	69
	Introduction	69
	Highlights of this Case Study	70
	SERD/CHHDC Population Movement	72
	Program Successes	77
	SERD/CHHDC Resident Employment and Earnings	78
	Urine Surveillance	80
	Comparative Cost Data: SERD/CHHDC and CTCY	81
	Evaluation	84
	Implications of this Case Study	88
	Proposed Plans For SERD/CHHDC for Fiscal Year 1973-1974	90

Appendix A	**Methodology Employed in the Case Study Evaluation**	97
	Introduction	97
	The Collection, Verification, and Presentation of Data for SERD/CHHDC	97
	The Presentation of Data in the Tables in this Report	99
Appendix B	**Glossary of Terms**	107
	Bibliography	109

Index 121

About the Authors 125

List of Figures

1-1	SERD/CHHDC Table of Organization	5
2-1	Range of Intensity of Evaluation	12
2-2	Examples of Areas to be Evaluated by Possible Levels of Intensity of the Evaluation	13
3-1	Intake Information Form	26
3-2	Resumé	28
3-3	Intake Form	29
3-4	Narrative Information	30
3-5	Family Information	35
3-6	Program Description Record	39
3-7	Resident Plan	40
3-8	Agreement	41
3-9	Career Plan	43
3-10	Parole Plan Form Letter	44
3-11	Notification of Parole Hearing: Residents	45
3-12	Notification of Parole Hearing: Nonresidents	46
3-13	Parole Progress Report	47
3-14	Follow-up Contact Form	49
3-15	Follow-up Report Form	50
4-1	MIS Report Form	63

4-2	MIS Weekly Summary Form	65
4-3	MIS Weekly Summary Form	65
4-4	MIS Quarterly Summary Form	67
4-5	MIS Annual Summary Form	68

List of Tables

5-1	SERD/CHHDC and CTCY Population Data by Resident Man-days for Quarter-years, FY 1972 and 1973	74
5-2	Population Movement: DCDC Youth Services Community Correctional Centers—FU1972	75
5-3	Population Movement: SERD/CHHDC and CTCY—FY 1973	76
5-4	Parole and Recidivism Data: SERD/CHHDC and CTCY	77
5-5	Time on Parole for SERD/CHHDC Parolees as of June 26, 1973	78
5-6	Comparison of SERD/CHHDC and CTCY Costs per Successful Parolee—FY 1973	82
5-7	Comparison of SERD/CHHDC and CTCY Costs per Man-day—FY 1973	83

Preface

A quiet revolution is underway in programs and services for incarcerated persons, mental patients, the mentally retarded, juvenile delinquents, drug addicts, alcoholics, and others who have social, personal, emotional, and physical problems that impede their adjustment to what is called "normal community life." Up to a few years ago, professionals, politicians, and most anyone concerned with problem people believed strongly that the most effective approach is to isolate them until at some magic point they would be "rehabilitated." Accordingly, prisons, mental hospitals, and other types of large, impersonal institutions were developed (usually in isolated areas) generally designed to "warehouse" unfortunate people.

The quiet revolution of moving people out of institutions and back to the community has taken several forms. Community-based treatment facilities are replacing prisons; community mental health centers, some of which are residential, are replacing mental health institutions. The community programs are variously called halfway houses, halfway-back houses, halfway-in houses, or community residential centers.

Institutions—as the solution for coping with problem people are increasingly being discredited. No longer do many responsible professionals believe that prisons rehabilitate criminals, that mental hospitals cure people with mental problems, that the retarded must be hidden away from society, or that juvenile delinquents can become normal adults if isolated from society during impressionable years. Also, institutions are expensive not only to construct, but to operate and maintain. In addition, what institutions really do is institutionalize people—that is, teach them to adjust to the institution rather than to the society to which a person must return if he or she is to be successfully rehabilitated.

The alternative to large, unattractive, isolated institutions has been to move the patient, the client, or other problem person as quickly as is possible back to the community from which he or she came, from which the problems originated and developed, and to which the person will ultimately return. The reason—aside from the fact that institutions do not cure—is simple: If a person is ever to return to family and community, this must be done by adjusting, not to an institution, but to that family and community.

There are no accurate estimates of the number of community-based treatment programs in the United States. There are probably more than 1,000 programs serving mental patients, retarded people, juvenile delinquents, alcoholics, drug users, convicts, and exconvicts. The number will grow in the future. The State of Massachusetts, for example, recently abolished all institutions serving juveniles. Other states have similar plans underway. Recent emphasis of many prison programs is on eliminating large prisons and developing community-based treatment facilities for convicts. Most states have established networks of community-based mental institutions to replace the turn-of-the-century mental hospitals. The growth in community programs in all areas is just now getting underway. There is no doubt that the use of community facilities will accelerate. This book focuses on one area—community treatment programs for offenders.

The basic characteristics of community-based programs are: First, they are not located in rural areas but rather in the neighborhoods and communities in which the clients live and eventually will return. A second characteristic is that they place a great deal of responsibility on the individual to work out solutions to his own problems. A third characteristic is that generally, the programs are small-scale efforts involving anywhere from a few individuals up to 30 to 60 at most. A fourth characteristic of community programs is that because they are located in a community setting, they involve community representatives in the programs in a variety of ways; employers, locally based social services, religious and neighborhood leaders, and others have new responsibilities and involvement with community programs. A fifth characteristic is that they stress rehabilitation. Institutions are concerned with maintenance. For example, prisons really do not try to rehabilitate prisoners. The major function of correctional institutions is to provide "room and board" and constant surveillance of the inmates. The opposite is the case with community programs: The stress is on rehabilitation and developing the skills and abilities of the client to function independently and effectively in the community. As a result, *all* staff and people involved in community correctional programs must focus on and be able to deal with the question of rehabilitation. A final characteristic of community programs is that they bring a variety of new people with new ideas to the rehabilitation effort. The emphasis of these programs is not so much on highly trained professionals and sophisticated professional approaches as on an ability to assist the client to resolve his or her own problems. Accordingly, many staff people in community correctional programs are exoffenders themselves and have been incarcerated in the same or similar institutions as the people they serve in the community center. Others are people with limited education but who have a great deal of rapport and empathy with residents of the center.

This book attempts to provide useful information, guidelines, and ideas for the evaluator of community treatment programs for offenders. It describes evaluation techniques and approaches and presents a case study of an internal evaluation produced by SERD of an experimental program operated effectively by the firm for over two years. This unique case study provides a comparative analysis of the privately operated SERD program with a similar program operated by a public agency. This book also contains an information system that was tested, refined, and used for over two years by SERD in the community program. This system provided a data base for evaluation, recorded basic characteristics and background information about residents, and plotted their progress through the program. This system provided the basis for numerous evaluations—both internal and external—conducted during the project.

John W. McCollum
President
SERD, Inc.

July 30, 1975

**Evaluating Community
Treatment Programs**

1 Introduction

Purposes of this Study

This study is a compilation of experience and information collected by staff of Social, Educational Research and Development, Inc. (SERD) in the evaluation of community correctional centers. It is designed to provide guidelines and examples for an individual or group charged with responsibility for evaluating a community correctional center program or program component. Included here are definitions, standards, examples, tools, techniques, guidelines, sample forms, and a bibliography, all of which should be useful to evaluators. The last chapter presents a case study of the evaluation of one center in which many of the tools and techniques were applied.

Later in this chapter the distinction between "evaluation" and "research" concerning social service programs is clarified. Essentially, "research" is concerned with basic issues of human behavior and the impact of institutions on human behavior, while "evaluation" focuses on particular programs, projects, or undertakings and asks highly specific questions about the effects and impacts of a program, such as, how does a program function, is it doing what it is supposed to be doing, is it producing successes, and what is the cost.

The purposes of this study are to show in step-by-step, concrete ways just what role "evaluation" plays in community correctional center programs and how evaluation can be effectively applied. Though evaluation is not research, it is important to understand what the limits of evaluations are, what it can and cannot do for a program, how it can be used, the conditions under which it should be applied, timing of evaluation studies, the role of evaluation, and the role of clients and what each should expect from the other. Other important issues are: who should conduct evaluation studies, data and information needs, tools for recording data and information, the cost of evaluation, how evaluation results should be reported, and a variety of other issues and questions that comprise an evaluation of community correctional center programs or activities.

Community Correctional Centers

Community correctional centers are often called halfway houses, halfway-in or halfway-out programs, community treatment centers, or community correctional centers. Sometimes they are quite restrictive in terms of the clients they serve.

Some programs serve only probationers or parolees while others serve offenders who are still under sentence. Some programs serve only women or only men while others are coed programs; some serve juveniles and others serve adults. Essentially, however, community correctional centers have the following basic characteristics.

1. They are oriented to rehabilitation as opposed to prisons which function largely to provide institutional or maintenance care for inmates.
2. They provide a variety of services generally focusing on integrating the individual into the community. These services include personal counseling, job placement, job counseling, family counseling, recreational services, education and training, loaning of funds, crisis intervention, assistance in finding housing, and residential care.
3. Community correctional centers are just what the term implies—community centers. They are located in the community and ideally provide the same kind of living arrangements in which the individual will live permanently once he or she is free of the system.

Community centers are not free of controversy. Because they are in the community, near where residents of varied socio-economic characteristics and opinions live, they often create a great deal of anxiety and hostility. Hardly a center has been established within the United States that has not been a target of considerable community attack. On the one hand, homeowners feel that community centers will lower property values and be a threat to the community or neighborhoods in which they are located. Others feel that community correctional centers are not the appropriate way to handle and/or treat offenders, convicts, or exconvicts. As a result of the controversy and hostility toward community centers, evaluation is an important tool and device because the community is constantly asking what the program is doing and how effectively is it accomplishing its goals.

The Role and Purposes of Evaluation

One of the most important roles of evaluation for community correctional centers is to establish the effectiveness of the program with the community and the funding agency. However, evaluation also is the most important technique available to assist in rational planning and in improving the effectiveness and efficiency of the program.

There is a difference between "evaluation" and "research." *The Dictionary of Behavioral Science* defines "evaluation" as the "determination of the relative value or importance of a score or phenomenon by appraisal or comparison with a standard."[1] On the other hand, the same dictionary defines "research" as "a detailed, systematic attempt, often prolonged, to discover or confirm through objective investigation the facts pertaining to a specified problem or problems and the laws and principles controlling it." Most community correctional centers will not have the financial and staff resources and expertise to undertake in-depth research activities relating to the program and/or the types of clients served. Therefore, evaluation is one of the most important ways for these programs to identify problems and priorities and plan a better and more effective program. Baseline data for comparative use should be collected beginning on the first day the center opens. If several programs receive support from the same funding source, this group should be able to conduct comparative analyses or provide data from other programs for use in evaluation activities.

Evaluation should serve at least five purposes for the community correctional center.

1. It should provide some measure of credibility for the program in the community and neighborhood where it is located.
2. It should provide information to the funding source regarding the extent to which the program is meeting its objectives and goals and thus provide a basis for increased funding or special activities.
3. It should provide management with an indication of program and staff strengths and weaknesses.
4. It should provide a link between staff performance and resident successes or failures.
5. It should suggest alternative courses of action and/or identify necessary program modifications.

SERD/CHHDC: A Community Treatment Center for Youthful Offenders

In June, 1971, Social, Educational Research and Development, Inc. (SERD), signed a contract with the District of Columbia Department of Corrections to operate a community-based treatment facility for convicted youthful felons, confined to the Department's two Youth Centers in Lorton, Virginia.[a] The contractor established a program called the SERD/Congress Heights Human Development Center. Many of the tools and techniques presented here in Chapters 2 and 3 were used in this Center during its two and one-half years of operation. The Management Information System (MIS) presented in Chapter 4 was used at the Center. Chapter 5 presents a case study evaluation of this Center conducted by SERD that demonstrates the utilization and application of many of the approaches and techniques suggested in this study.

SERD/CHHDC was located at 406 Condon Terrace, S.E., Washington, D.C.,

[a]The contract was for a three-year period to be renewed annually.

in a renovated 14-unit apartment building. According to D.C. housing regulations, the facility could accommodate a maximum of 84 residents; the Certificate of Occupancy was for an average of 55 residents. Some space was set aside for recreational areas, staff offices, storage, etc.

The organizational structure of the Center was described in the SERD/CHHDC Policy Statement submitted in 1972 to the Department of Corrections.[2] Essentially, the staff was organized into two major divisions. One division, known as the "Program Services Division," provided all resident treatment and rehabilitation services. The Division was under the direction of the Chief of Programs. Reporting to him were counselors who had primary responsibility for counseling, guidance, and working with residents in terms of employment, education, drug problems, and the like. This staff also had responsibility for recording most of the information required by the Management Information System (MIS) and on other forms and records. The second division was the "Operations Division" and was supervised by the Chief of Operations. This Division provided management support, 24-hour supervisory responsibility, and housekeeping services for the staff, internal evaluation, security of the facility, maintenance of the Center and its grounds, the conduct and supervision of urine surveillance programs, development and implementation of contracts for the improvement and maintenance of the grounds and facilities, record-keeping including establishment and maintenance of individual resident files, operation of the food program and kitchen, handling of the petty cash and resident loan funds, preparation of reports, maintenance of records, provision of messenger services, and provision of secretarial services to all staff. Figure 1-1 presents the organizational structure of the Center.

The major thrust of the SERD/CHHDC counseling program was to provide the direction, stimuli, and support necessary to assist residents in securing employment (or to enroll in an appropriate training or educational program), to remain drug-free, and to plan and prepare for release or parole. The following are essentially the goals the Department of Corrections had established for community centers.

1. Staff of the center should provide residents with assistance in getting jobs and/or enrolling in career, education, or training programs.
2. Residents should demonstrate that they are able to stay free of drugs during their stay at the Center.
3. The Center should ensure that residents develop suitable living arrangements for use after they leave the Center.
4. Residents should demonstrate that they are able to establish useful interpersonal relations and effectively manage their own behavior during their stay in the Center.

Ultimately, then, the *test of effectiveness of the program was the extent to*

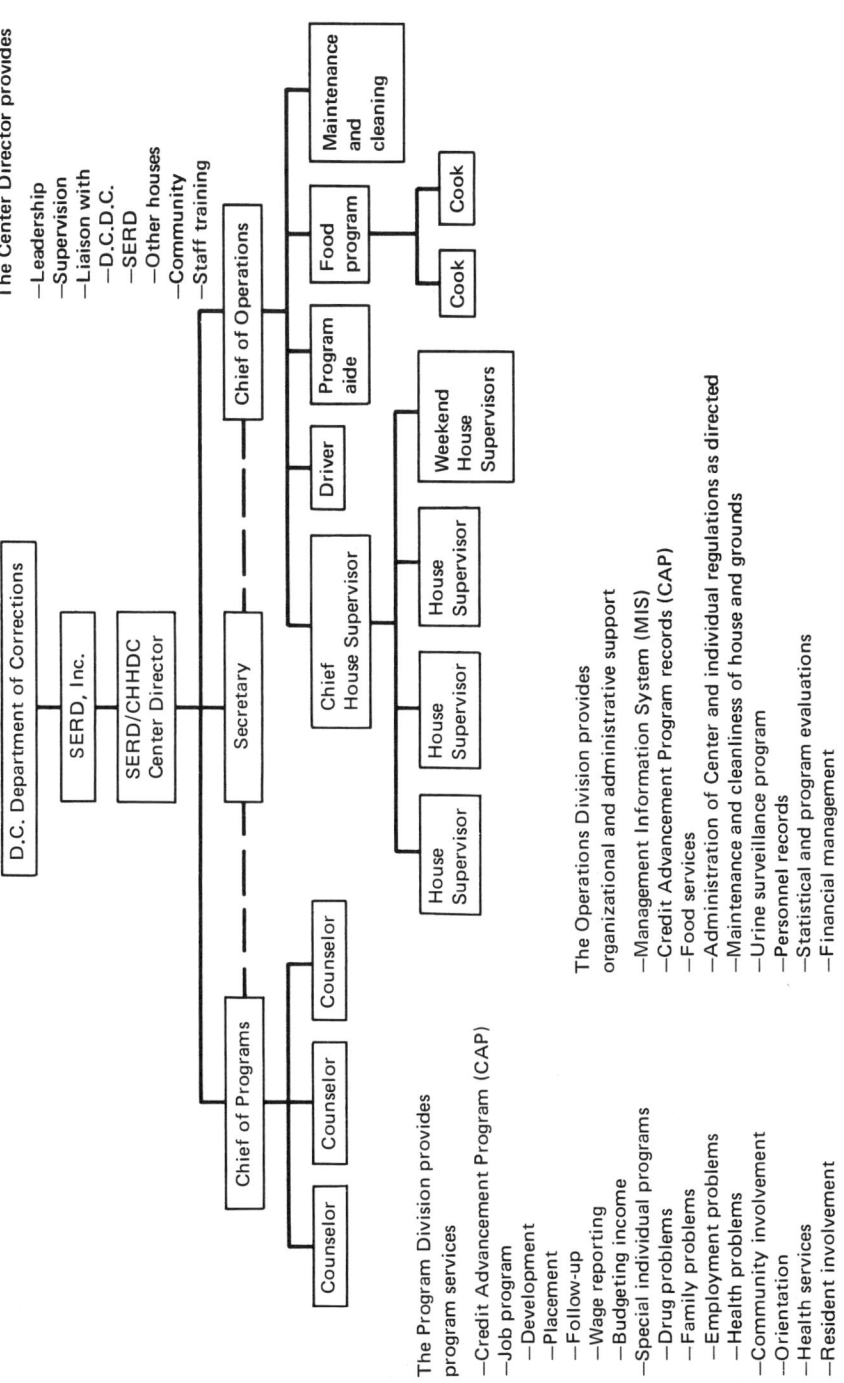

Figure 1-1. SERD/CHHDC Table of Organization

which young men passing through the Center could remain crime-free. This was the basic goal to which this project addressed itself.[b]

While in the Center, residents were preoccupied with the problems of adjusting to the free world, i.e., avoiding drugs, getting and holding a decent job, and establishing effective interpersonal relations. These were the problems on which the counseling program focused; the reality of the present world was clear. To qualify for parole, residents must have demonstrated their ability to hold a job or remain in a training or education program; they must have demonstrated their ability to readjust to the community, their family, and friends; they must have been able to appropriately use community resources; and they must have resolved drug problems. The Center functioned to help residents achieve these goals on a relatively short-term basis and at the same time to provide the kind of reinforcement that would enhance their chances of maintaining constructive behavior.

As noted, SERD/CHHDC, served a maximum of 55 residents on a residential basis. In addition, a maximum of 25 residents were served on an "out-count" (out-patient) basis. The residents moved through the program on the basis of satisfactorily completing five stages in the Credit Advancement Program (CAP) which was a modified behavior-modification program. The length of time residents spent in residence varied but averaged about seven to ten weeks. Upon completion of the "in-count" stage, residents moved to "out-count." The average length of time in out-count status before parole ranged from several weeks to several months.

CAP consisted of five phases, briefly as follows.

Phase I: Orientation. During this period the resident's behavior was monitored, and individual records were maintained on his performance. All residents remained in Phase I for two weeks.

Phase II: Early Rehabilitation Phase. During this period residents began to earn credits to advance to the next phase. Minimum time in this phase was one week. To move to Phase III, residents must have earned 100 individual and 35 group credits, be employed, and give urines as required.

Phase III: Intermediate Rehabilitation Phase. To advance to Phase IV, residents must have earned a minimum of 100 individual and 35 group credits for a two-week period, must remain employed, and must give urines as required.

Phase IV: Advanced Rehabilitation Phase. During this phase residents received counseling on the responsibilities of out-count living. To move to Phase V

---

[b]Residents were all innercity youths averaging between 18 through 24 years of age. The majority were convicted felons with criminal justice contacts dating back to when they were 10 to 12 years of age. Most had considerable "hard drug" experience.

(out-count) a resident must have earned credits as noted in Phase III, remain employed, give urine as required, and demonstrate that he had suitable living arrangements for out-count.

Phase V: Out-count. While on out-count, residents were required to maintain employment (education and/or training), stay drug-free, and report regularly to the Center. This was the final phase of the program.

When residents arrived at SERD/CHHDC, they were under sentence (Federal Youth Corrections Act) and remained in that status until parole was granted. Accordingly, residents who failed in the program (inability or refusal to work, rearrest, drug usage, excessive rule violations, etc.) could be returned to the institution.

During FY 1973, a number of new programs were instituted at SERD/CHHDC.

1. A Management Information System (MIS) was put into operation. This program was based on the collection of detailed data on such activities as the urine surveillance program, employment, and resident adjustment. The MIS is presented in Chapter 4. The MIS, revised once in 1972 and again in 1973, proved very effective in tracking the progress and problems of residents, identifying residents who were apt to develop problems, comparing staff and program effectiveness in dealing with residents, and focusing on special problems, such as drugs and employment. This MIS (as of June 1973) was the only such system in operation in a community-based treatment facility anywhere in the country (to SERD's knowledge).

2. The Credit Advancement Program (CAP) was implemented in 1972 and was a modified behavior-modification program that rewarded residents for positive behavior and charted their progress through five stages in the Center. It was revised several times and worked most effectively as a treatment approach.

3. The Urine Surveillance Program presented a continuing problem at SERD/CHHDC caused by delays in receiving results from the laboratory. Accordingly, in 1972, a private contract was undertaken with a local laboratory to provide urine surveillance services on a supplemental basis. When residents were suspected of using drugs and staff felt it necessary to get a quick "reading" on a resident, a daily urine sample was taken and submitted to the laboratory, which provided a 24-hour, or same-day response. This proved to be effective in monitoring and controlling drug problems of Center residents.

4. When the Center was first organized, a community policy committee was organized to guide the project. In the spring of 1972, the chairman resigned and the committee disintegrated. In view of the fact that the Center (in spring, 1973) was well established in the community and accepted by it, a different approach was planned for the utilization of committees and for community input. This consisted of establishing a series of task groups that would focus on specific problem areas within the SERD/CHHDC program. These task forces, however, did not get underway prior to December, 1974, when the center closed.

5. In the spring of 1973, a detailed Procedures Manual was developed for use by staff as an orientation and training tool for new staff and to reduce all operating procedures of the Center to writing so that staff would know exactly what action must be taken in day-to-day operations or when emergencies arose.[3]

6. Community involvement activities during 1972-1973 included a Thanksgiving Eve banquet for residents and staff and their families. As part of the effort to reach out into the community, in December, 1972, the staff sponsored a Christmas party for 50 teenagers in the surrounding neighborhood. Food and soft drinks were served, and each youth was presented with a gift donated by local merchants. Staff members from a community youth program and members of the Community Relations Division of the Metropolitan Police Department also participated in this event.

7. In late 1972, two staff members were instrumental in organizing a SERD/CHHDC basketball team. The team played in a series of tournaments, and while their won-lost record was something less than .500, it provided a constructive activity for the ten residents participating. Uniforms were purchased, and the SERD/CHHDC van was used to transport the team to and from the games that were played in Virginia, the District of Columbia, and Maryland.

It was SERD's policy to employ staff with the highest potential for service and continued growth rather than only employing people with extensive previous experience. In several instances, personnel had not had extensive formal training. For example, the President of The Inner Voices of Lorton (an inmate of the Lorton Reformatory who organized The Inner Voices to involve inmates in creative dramatic and related activities for presentation in the community) was assigned to SERD/CHHDC as a resident to work part-time in community development activities. Some house supervisors and counselors were former inmates at Lorton who had demonstrated successful rehabilitation. In addition to this, SERD/CHHDC implemented new, innovative, and advanced programs that required understanding if they were to be effective. Therefore, a program was established to continually upgrade staff competence through meetings, seminars, and/or individual educational programs and staff counseling sessions.

During 1972-1973, SERD/CHHDC staff participated in the following training programs.

1. An educational consultant was employed to provide training for the counseling staff in writing and progress report preparation.
2. The staff of Behavioral Technology Consultants, Inc., were available on an ongoing basis for staff training to implement and monitor the Credit Advancement Program. Six training sessions were held in fall, 1972, in connection with initial implementation of the program, and additional sessions held in spring, 1973, provided training in CAP revisions and in consolidation of the CAP form with MIS forms.
3. Three advanced students from the Center for Group Studies of the Psychi-

atric Institute Foundation coled (with staff counselors) resident counseling groups at SERD/CHHDC.
4. The Director, all counselors, and two part-time staff were enrolled on a full or part-time basis in undergraduate and graduate studies at Federal City College, Howard University, The George Washington University, and The Johns Hopkins University.
5. All staff met in a weekly three-hour, in-service staff training program.

This project and the effectiveness of these approaches and activities are described in greater detail in the case study presented in Chapter 5.

How to Use this Study

There are five important features to this study of evaluation procedures.

First, the study discusses the pitfalls and problems of the evaluation of community correctional centers—specifically, how evaluation should be used, the manner in which it should be used, how it should be conducted, and the specific steps that should be followed.

Second: Perhaps the basic problem in conducting evaluations is that few programs have even minimal data. For example, the authors have seen case file after case file that omits such basic data as personal background characteristics, the plan developed for a given resident, and the extent to which the plan was achieved. Chapters 3 and 4 contain a variety of processes, techniques, forms, information systems, etc.—tools that are not in themselves evaluative techniques but which if utilized, will go a long way toward alleviating the data gaps that usually exist in community centers.

Third, a case study is included of one community correctional center that portrays how a complete evaluation design was implemented in one program. The case study moves the reader through the entire process of how the evaluation was designed, the questions it was supposed to answer, the techniques used to get the answers, and the conclusions and recommendations that resulted from the evaluation.

Fourth, the study contains a sample format for a management information system that was tested and used in a community correctional center program that operated for over two years. This system provided the data base necessary to complete evaluations of resident movement and progress and staff effectiveness.

Fifth, the study contains a bibliography that is representative of useful literature in the field compiled to assist an evaluator of community correctional programs. The bibliography is not all-inclusive, nor is it limited to the field of correctional programs. It is designed to guide the evaluator in searching for new techniques and approaches that could be applicable to evaluations of community correctional center programs.

The reader who is interested only in the case study of how an evaluation was actually conducted should read Chapter 5. The reader who is interested in designing a complete evaluation system for a community correctional center should read Chapters 2, 3, and 4. Program staff and administrators who are interested in designing and implementing an information system that will provide baseline data for future evaluations should read Chapter 4.

Notes

1. Benjamin B. Wolman, ed., *Dictionary of Behavioral Science* (New York: Van Nostrand Reinhold and Company, 1973).

2. See SERD, Inc., "Policies and Procedures Statement for the Operation of SERD/Congress Heights Human Development Center (CHHDC) During the Second Year," submitted to D.C. Department of Corrections, July, 1972, 17 pages.

3. SERD, Inc., *A Procedures Manual for the SERD/Congress Heights Human Development Center* (Washington, D.C.: SERD, Inc., May 10, 1973).

2 Designing and Using Evaluation Systems and Techniques

The General Setting

Whether stated specifically, evaluations must start with the question: What is this program supposed to accomplish? This is a relatively simple question in education, for example, but not necessarily in the criminal justice and rehabilitation fields. Basic evaluation problems in the correctional rehabilitation field are the elusive nature of crime, its resolution, and its causes; the difficulty in measuring crime; the differences in treatment modalities and program operation and management; and the differences in characteristics, background, education, and socio-economic status of individuals convicted of the same crime, to name a few. Very simply and briefly stated, these problems include the following issues.

1. The causes of crime are matters of speculation. There is no agreement that criminal behavior has any single or even combination of causes. Generally, most experts in the field agree that criminal behavior is related to discrimination, certain age groups, the organization of society, poverty, unemployment, and a variety of other factors. However, agreement breaks down in terms of the mix of and relative importance of these components.
2. Activities perceived as crime are not universally agreed upon by all in society. Groups, individuals, and even jurisdictions define crime, as well as the seriousness of a given offense, differently.
3. Many remedies for crime are outside the responsibility and control of criminal justice agencies. Thus it is one thing to talk about reducing crime and still another to assign this responsibility to the police or to a correctional agency that may have responsibilities for custody, apprehension, rehabilitation, and detection of crime rather than prevention.
4. The variables and mix of circumstances necessary for a person to remain free of criminal activities are not the same in each case and, in many cases, cannot be determined in the short time the individual may spend in a community correctional center.
5. The roles played by staff, friends, family, peers, and others in the adjustment and rehabilitation process are not always identifiable.
6. Community centers vary considerably in terms of treatment approach, type of facilities, staff expertise, management approaches, types of clients, etc., which cause problems in terms of comparing one center or program component with another.

Given these broad problems, the general goal of community correctional centers is to focus on two aspects of rehabilitation: (1) to assist the offender in adjusting to the community and atmosphere where he will eventually reside, and (2) to assist the resident in equipping himself or herself with the skills, knowledge, and goals necessary to remain free of the criminal justice system in the future. Measuring effectiveness in these areas is extremely difficult. Generally, this requires sophisticated behavioral science, psychological, and other methodological tools and procedures that may not be available. The cost to measure effectiveness is also high. Methodological approaches available, such as longitudinal analysis, pre and postprogram analysis, and control group analysis require a degree of sophistication and often a length of time to complete that are not available nor reasonable in community programs. Thus, given these broad operational problems, determining the kind and level of evaluation, defining objectives, determining the data requirements and methods of analysis, selecting the methods for measuring impact, and determining the scope of evaluation are often difficult and sophisticated problems.

Kinds and Levels of Evaluation

The range of kinds and levels of evaluation which can be undertaken in community correctional programs varies along a scale of increasing intensity. For instance, at one extreme is the limited, "one-shot" approach which might focus on a specific area or program component and be completed in a short period of time ranging from a few hours to a few days. At the other extreme are extensive, in-depth, or full-scale, evaluations that focus on the total program, several components, or a large-scale problem and that may be completed over a long period of time, ranging from several months to several years. Between these two extremes are innumerable mixes of types and levels of evaluation that can be conducted in a community correctional center. If this range of intensity is assumed to exist, it might look something like the scale in Figure 2-1 which assumes a range with five levels of intensity.

The chart in Figure 2-2 presents a partial list of some components, records, and activities in a community correctional center that might be evaluated and an

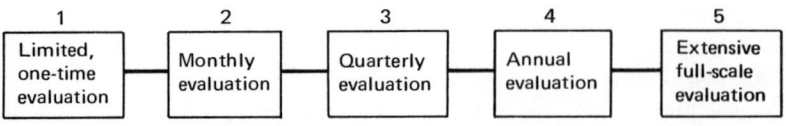

Figure 2-1. Range of Intensity of Evaluation

| | Intensity of evaluation |||||
Areas for possible evaluation	1	2	3	4	5
1. Staff personnel records			X	X	
2. Client files		X	X		
3. Client loan fund		X	X		
4. Client progress reports		X	X		X
5. Supporting services	X		X	X	X
6. Treatment assessment	X		X	X	X
7. Staffing patterns	X			X	X
8. Program services	X			X	X
9. Counseling techniques	X			X	X
10. Management of the Center	X				X
11. Relations with the broader community	X				X
12. Job-development activities	X				X
13. Fiscal audit	X	X	X	X	X
14. Furnishings and facility appearance	X		X		X
15. Follow-up of former clients	X		X	X	X

Figure 2-2. Examples of Areas to be Evaluated by Possible Levels of Intensity of the Evaluation

indication of the levels of evaluation from the range noted in Figure 2-1 that might be applied. Each component, activity, or record listed could be evaluated at one or more levels. The level of intensity of the evaluation should be determined early in the planning stages. It should be determined by the cost involved, manpower requirements, expected results, and reasons for evaluating this particular area.

These levels or kinds of evaluation undertaken in community correctional centers may be conducted either internally or by independent, third-party evaluators. External, or third-party, evaluations are generally conducted if any one of three conditions exist:

1. the staff lacks the competence or expertise in the specific area to be evaluated,
2. an evaluation of a particular area conducted internally would be suspect or lack credibility, or
3. an evaluation of a particular area conducted internally would probably result in division among the staff.

Four types of evaluation are noted below that are appropriate for most community correctional centers. These include a mix of internal and external evaluations in a wide variety of areas and which are conducted for various time periods throughout the operation of the center. The reader should bear in mind that this represents only one possible approach to planning the types and levels of evaluation for a community correctional center program.

1. Ongoing Internal Evaluation. A community center cannot operate successfully and effectively without some form of ongoing internal evaluation. This type of evaluation provides early detection and self-corrective mechanisms to identify what is wrong, to determine how the center is achieving written goals and objectives, and to provide trend data and information for planning purposes. Internal evaluation might be conducted by a community advisory committee, staff, or the sponsoring agency. It may involve residents, staff, the community, or only files and records. Ongoing evaluation should provide for regular reviews of special areas and spot checking of other areas that may identify problems or provide suggestions for improvement. Some areas that might receive ongoing internal evaluation include meeting curfews by residents, job-development activities by staff, frequency with which residents take advantage of job leads and/or change jobs, petty cash fund, resident loan fund, meal planning, attendance at meals, staff performance, record-keeping and reporting.

2. Scheduled Periodic Internal Evaluation. This type of evaluation usually is conducted on a regular cycle (i.e., monthly, quarterly, semi-annually, or annually) and focuses on specific program areas to determine operational effectiveness. These evaluations are usually conducted by senior project and/or management staff and provide valuable guidance for planning. Some areas that might be included in evaluations of this sort are: cohort analyses of length of time in program for residents and final disposition, comparative analyses of caseloads, audits of petty cash and loan funds, formal staff performance evaluations, reviews of goals and objectives resulting in modifications or amendments based on past performance, comparisons of effectiveness of counseling techniques based on resident problems and/or background.

3. External or Third-party Evaluation. At least once a year, usually coordinated with the funding cycle, the total operation of a center should be thoroughly assessed. It is wise for these assessments to be conducted on a regular and systematic annual basis. This outside independent evaluation should cost about 5 percent or less of the operating costs for the year. It should be conducted by an individual or firm independent of the project. The evaluator should submit a written proposal and budget for the project. A formal review process for selection of the evaluator should be undertaken by the program staff and a representative of the funding agency for the project, if appropriate. This evaluation may focus on different aspects of the program, i.e., the first year evaluation might focus on overall management and staff performance, the second year focus might be on program activities and services to residents, and the third year might focus on a process analysis. An alternative to this, or in addition to it, the entire program could be evaluated from the standpoint of overall effectiveness and cost. If other similar programs operate in the same locality, it may be possible to conduct sophisticated cost-benefit analyses and comparative recidivism studies. This, however, requires careful planning and a detailed evaluation design that must be carried out over a long period of time.

4. Intensive, Unscheduled External Evaluation. This type of evaluation should be conducted at times when management staff need to know the effectiveness of a program component or are trying to solve a particular problem. This type of evaluation is best conducted by a single individual who has particular expertise in the area to be evaluated. For example, the management staff may want to know if group counseling is more effective with certain types of residents than is individual counseling, if other management approaches might be more effective, how family counseling sessions could be strengthened and made more effective, or how to develop and carry out follow-up procedures for former residents.

Selecting an Outside Evaluator

Evaluation in action settings is difficult and demanding; it calls for a great deal of imagination and tenacity, as well as research ability. The reason an evaluation report is poor or mediocre may be due in part to the abilities and/or expertise of the consultant or group conducting the evaluation.

In selecting an outside evaluator who is unknown to project staff or who is new to the field, the following should be considered.

1. Has the evaluator conducted similar studies in criminal justice or related fields?
2. Has the evaluator been eager and timely in providing references, samples of previous work, or other information requested?
3. Has the client staff been able to establish effective interpersonal relations with the evaluator?
4. Has the evaluator treated confidences of previous clients discreetly in his discussions?
5. Has the evaluator provided a professionally written plan for conducting the study, a plan that specifies the problem, the methods and procedures to be used, the cost, and a specific timetable?
6. Does the evaluator recognize the need for staff to be involved in solving their problems and those of the program?
7. Does the evaluator avoid negative criticism of other evaluators or of evaluations conducted previously of this program?
8. Has the client staff reviewed the résumé or corporate capability statements

of the evaluator, and are they satisfied with the technical competence of the evaluator?
9. Has the evaluator been courteous, honest, and nonobtrusive in preliminary meetings, discussions with staff, and in visits to the program, to the best of the client's knowledge?
10. Is the evaluator willing to have his services evaluated through feedback, regular progress meetings, etc.?

If answers to each of the ten questions is unequivocally, "yes," the evaluator is probably worthy of final consideration. There are no set guidelines for assessing the evaluator's capabilities, but the preceding ten questions should provide areas for discussion and assessment by the project staff or potential client during the selection process.

Once the evaluator has been selected, all terms and conditions of the agreement should be in writing, preferably in the form of a binding contract which describes exactly what will be provided, under what terms, at what cost, and the commitments of both parties. Both parties should sign the agreement. In the event a formal contract is not desired (usually when the study is a minor effort), at a minimum, memoranda of agreement should be exchanged. The funding source should protect its investment by requiring written progress reports prior to payments and the submission of a final report before making final payment. Some organizations may prefer financial penalties to be assessed against the evaluator for nonperformance or for failure to meet time schedules.

Cost of Evaluation

Each community correctional center should budget some amount of money for evaluation each funding period. The amount may be small the first year and be increased as the program receives funding in subsequent years. The amount should be determined based on the extent, scope, and level of intensity of evaluation planned to be completed during each funding period.

There are no set guidelines for determining the amount of money to be earmarked for evaluation. It depends on the amount of funds available, the level of operations, the treatment approach used, the extent of in-house expertise in the areas to be evaluated, and the proposed evaluation plan. All of these considerations should be a part of the planning, budgeting, and negotiating processes.

SERD suggests 3 to 7 percent of total operating costs as a reasonable guideline for programs to consider after other considerations have been met. A minimum of $2,500 is necessary for any substantive evaluation. This is not to suggest that "evaluation" should be last to be considered and usually too late at that for its piece of the money pie. In fact, evaluation has in some cases not only proven effective in establishing a program's credibility in the community and with social service and funding agencies, but it has also provided extended life for some centers by providing a sound basis for continued funding.

Methods and Techniques in Conducting Evaluations

All the types of evaluation noted earlier should be part of the overall evaluation theme for a community correctional center. Irrespective of the type of evaluation being undertaken, several basic steps should be followed in conducting the evaluation. These steps are presented here and represent the range of activities—all may not be necessary or appropriate for each type of evaluation described earlier.

Step 1. Select the area of focus of the evaluation and define the limits and scope. These should be concise and put in writing.

Step 2. Determine the group or records to be studied and select the study period. The study period may follow the limits of the funding year or be selected based on other considerations. For example, if the study involves follow-up or recidivism studies, the study period should be one for which all residents served during that period have had little or no contact with the program for at least six months.

Step 3. Identify the specific methods and techniques to be used in conducting the evaluation and put these in writing. Some methods and techniques that might be considered include the following:

a. sampling,
b. personal interviews,
c. group interviews,
d. confidential interview guides or questionnaires completed during, before, or after personal interviews,
e. mail surveys,
f. telephone surveys,
g. pre and postanalyses of data and information,
h. individual observations of meetings, sessions, daily activities, weekend activities, etc.,
i. financial reviews or audits,
j. specification and measurement of objectives,
k. site visits,
l. use of control groups,

m. comparisons with baseline and/or national data,
n. team observation,
o. literature search, and
p. case studies.

Several methods and techniques should be selected to provide independent validity checks for the evaluator. The methods should provide both quantitative and qualitative data and information, especially if the evaluation is broad in scope and near the "extensive" level of intensity on the scale noted earlier.

Step 4. Determine the evaluation plan and commit this to writing. The plan should include the focus of the study, the group to be studied, the study period, methods to be used in the evaluation, a timetable for completion, any special requirements or requests to be made of project staff, residents or others, and a description of the final product to be produced.

Step 5. Review the evaluation plan with appropriate project staff and the funding agency and obtain their approval of the Plan *prior* to starting the evaluation.

Step 6. Collect data, conduct interviews, complete survey research, and review materials. This step is essentially the completion of the data collection requirements in the plan noted in Step 4. It is important that some validity checks of data be conducted. These might include rechecking files, matching community characteristics with census data, conducting a second interview, and other approaches. The evaluation plan should specify how validity will be determined.

Step 7. Analyze data and information and prepare a draft report. Specific conclusions and recommendations should flow from the data analysis stage and should be presented in the report. An outline of the report should be approved in advance by the funding source. Data and information may be presented in the report in narrative summary or through the use of tables, statistical charts, graphs, and/or a combination of these. Photographs, overlays, and other techniques may be used. The writer should present the report in such a way that it will be understood easily and will be useful and helpful to his client. This goal should determine the style, format, and elaborateness of the report.

Step 8. Submit draft report to project staff and/or funding agency for their comments and critique. If possible, request that the draft also be reviewed by a minimum of one and a maximum of three outside independent reviewers selected because of their expertise or knowledge of the field.

Step 9. Reduce the report to final form and submit multiple copies to the client. The evaluator may also prepare a brief three- to four-page "executive summary" if the report is unusually long and complicated or if the report is designed for wide distribution. It should be noted that some levels and types of evaluation—at the "limited" extreme of the level-of-intensity range—may only require an oral report, a memo to the Center Director, or a brief-letter report. In this case, Steps 7 and 8 would be omitted from the evaluation process.

Step 10. If possible, an outside evaluator may want to provide one to three days of postevaluation consultant time to assist staff in implementing recommendations in the report.

Expectations of Evaluations

Essentially, evaluative studies should describe and document the extent, nature, and scope of a program's effectiveness and efficiency. Evaluations should answer questions about which components of a program did what to whom, and under what circumstances.

Despite general agreement that usually exists regarding the purposes of evaluation, it is nevertheless necessary to clearly establish agreement between the evaluator and the client regarding exactly what the study will produce in terms of the reliability and validity of the results. For example, evaluation results are generally limited by all or some of the following factors:

1. the availability of data,
2. kinds of data,
3. cooperation by the staff,
4. cost,
5. response rates,
6. rapport between the evaluator and his client,
7. time period involved,
8. experience, competence, and expertise of the evaluator,
9. level and kinds of evaluation to be conducted, and
10. expectations of client and evaluator.

For the reasons noted, expectations must not be too ambitious or sophisticated for the limitations placed on the study. The basic rationale for conducting evaluation studies of community correctional centers is to provide information for action, to confirm what is suspected, and/or to provide information that contributes to planning and decision-making. Therefore, for the project to be worthwhile, the results should get a fair hearing, and the recommendations should be at least reviewed and considered.

Planners and evaluators should be aware of the problems and limitations of evaluation studies. In some cases, a final report may be too abstract and theoretical for use in the form received. The study may have been poorly defined and the conduct loosely managed. Some evaluation studies are not precise or specific but instead present the material in a global or theoretical form. Many of these pitfalls can be avoided through careful planning and if the evaluator and the client both understand clearly "why" the evaluation is being conducted. Evaluators should also attempt to fully understand the organization involved, its decision-making processes, and the people involved as staff and residents. This careful planning and understanding of the situation should provide a final evaluation report that can add its weight to a thrust for change toward better or different ways of operation and the provision of services to clients.

The program staff and/or funding agency may have a number of expectations about the conduct of the evaluation as well as of the outcome. Expectations regarding the conduct of the evaluation may be the most difficult for the evaluator to handle. For example, staff may all expect to have some appropriate input; they may expect the evaluator to conduct himself in a businesslike manner; they may expect the evaluation to be completed by a certain target date; or they may expect to actively participate in the evaluation. On the other hand, staff may expect the evaluator to "find out for himself" all the facts and decide not to help him; they may resent the evaluator's presence during staff meetings, counseling sessions, etc.; and they may be opposed to the reasons for undertaking the evaluation. The evaluator must be aware of these attitudes as early as possible during the planning stages. It is important that the attitudes and expectations of staff be considered by the evaluator when the evaluation design is prepared. Confidential information must be protected; staff who are hostile must be convinced to cooperate, if possible; and the activities of the evaluator should be carried out in a professional, nonobtrusive manner. If the evaluator is not able to establish his credibility with the staff, the evaluation could be seriously impaired.

Expectations about outcomes may be easier for the evaluator to handle because he or she will have an opportunity to work with the staff during the evaluation, to share findings briefly along the way, and to establish credibility. If this has occurred and the findings are supported by precise documentation, the evaluator should experience minimum difficulties in getting clients to accept the validity of conclusions. The conclusions may represent the suspicions of staff that have now been verified, or they may be different from the initially expected outcomes. However, the effectiveness of the evaluator in presenting conclusions will be dependent primarily on the ability of the evaluator to present a well-documented case and upon rapport already established between the staff and the evaluator.

Another important expectation in evaluation is presentation of suggestions, recommendations, and/or innovative ideas. Program staff generally expect the evaluator to specify alternative courses or to make suggestions and recommendations based on conclusions reached during the evaluation. Recommendations should be realistic, specific, and workable. If alternative courses are presented, these should be clearly stated and justified based on the findings of the evaluation. Recommendations, suggestions, or alternatives should be discussed in advance with program staff to determine their reactions and to determine the extent to which these suggestions are realistic for the project. The evaluator who ignores this important last step does not complete the job and shirks, in part, the responsibility to the client.

A final point about the acceptance of recommendations. Evaluative studies (unless they are a "whitewash") are more often than not a threat to some program staff who have strong personal and career identifications with their programs and/or clients and to administrators who must justify programs. Thus, when evaluations clash with cherished positions, the evaluation often will be denounced and attempts will be made to discredit it. Evaluators must expect this and be prepared to defend their reports; on the other hand, clients should require and expect an honest evaluation. An "honest evaluator" will give an "honest evaluation," but some ways of softening the "blow" to the client and assuring "honest" results are:

1. Make sure both the client and evaluator clearly understand and agree on the goals and objectives of the evaluation before it begins.
2. Give the client advance warning of threatening conclusions and recommendations; hopefully, changes will be implemented before the study results are available.
3. Let the client review a preliminary draft of the final report and if the evaluator is unwilling to change the report as requested by the client, indicate this in the report and explain why.
4. Require the client to put all his criticisms of the preliminary draft report in writing; many criticisms may seem less serious when viewed on paper.
5. Instead of making suggested changes, offer the client the option of including in the report (as an appendix) his written critique.
6. Submit to the client a list of independent reviewers (to review the draft report) and ask the client to select the reviewer(s). Include the written comments of the independent reviewer(s) in the final report.

Issues in the Evaluation of Community Correctional Centers

Evaluation of community correctional centers should focus on specific issues. Some important issues are:

1. length of time residents should spend in the program,
2. the most effective counseling techniques for specific problems,

3. the implications of excessive curfew violations by residents,
4. the significance of education, employment, and/or training as determinants for success,
5. the reasons for particular rates of recidivism among certain groups of residents,
6. whether the effectiveness of staff is a factor in determining resident success or failure,
7. whether the physical facility, community, and/or neighborhood play a role in the adjustment of residents,
8. whether the management and staffing patterns of the center are effective and important,
9. whether the cost of producing a successful resident is different for different groups of residents and why,
10. whether the cost of center operations are comparable to costs of other similar programs,
11. whether the cost per successful resident is increasing or decreasing and why,
12. whether previous experience, education, and/or length of time on the job make staff members more or less effective,
13. whether the program of activities and treatment program are appropriate in meeting the needs of the resident population,
14. the impact of family members and/or relevant others on the resident's adjustment,
15. the attitudes of the community and neighborhood toward the program and center,
16. the impact of drug or alcohol use on residents' abilities to adjust,
17. types of follow-up support or techniques that are more effective than others,
18. the types of supporting services from outside agencies that are necessary and effective with this group,
19. activities that volunteers pursue more effectively than staff and whether these should be undertaken, and
20. the impact of the center in bringing about institutional and community change.

These issues are representative of those that should be considered by programs and funding agencies of community correctional centers. The issues for a particular program will depend on the type of treatment program used, the characteristics of residents served, staffing patterns, the condition and location of the physical facility, and many other factors too numerous to mention. If the issues have not been conceptualized and established prior to the evaluation, the evaluator will have no guidelines or parameters, and the funding sources will undoubtedly be disappointed in the final product.

3 Forms and Procedures

Introduction

This chapter describes and includes samples of basic forms, procedures, and systems necessary to providing an adequate data base for evaluation. Many programs studied by SERD have not established information systems nor have they developed basic forms and procedures to make possible the collection and maintenance of information on clients served during the time they are in the program and for a follow-up period. Chapter 4 presents a Management Information System (MIS) that was used by SERD for over two years and that tracks residents or clients in a program.

Written Procedures Manual

It is suggested that programs produce a "Policy and Procedures Manual" that describes all aspects of program operation and that contains forms, report formats, and plans for organization of case and other files, and any other such information necessary for a smooth-operating program. A manual will not only aid staff in fulfilling their duties and responsibilities more efficiently and serve as a staff training tool, but it will also provide a standard, guideline, and basis for evaluating staff performance and program performance. It will also make it possible for an outside evaluator to critically assess program and management procedures and make recommendations for improvements or changes.

    The manual should be assembled in a manner to facilitate changes, additions, and deletions. All full-time staff members should have a copy of the manual at their work station, and one senior staff person should be designated responsibility for keeping all copies current. One copy should also be placed at the work station of the person "on duty" if other than a senior staff member.

    The manual should be all-inclusive in that it should cover procedures to be followed in the event of any emergency, resident change in status, etc. It should also include a description of such items as the staffing patterns and treatment approach utilized in the project. It should contain a copy of all forms and an explanation for initiating, completing, and distributing required forms and reports. It should identify all program and management responsibilities for each position title. A suggested outline for such a procedures manual follows.

I. Table of Contents
II. Introduction and Purpose of the Manual
III. General Behavior of Staff, Residents, and Guests in the Center
IV. Organizational Structure of the Program
V. Telephone Directory of Frequently Used Numbers
VI. Emergencies
    A. Fire
    B. Riot or Civil Disturbances
    C. Medical Problems
    D. Thefts
VII. Duty Officer Procedures
VIII. Glossary of Commonly Used Program Terms
IX. Most Recent Program Design (Approved by the Funding Agency or Currently in Use)
X. Treatment Program Procedures
XI. Resident Procedures and Accountability
    A. Intake Procedures
    B. Orientation
    C. Maintenance of Residents' Personal Belongings
    D. Procedures for Sign-in and Sign-out of Residents
    E. Drug/Alcohol Urine Surveillance Programs
    F. Employment/Education or Training Programs
    G. Attendance at Group Meetings
    H. Rearrest Procedures
    I. Transfer Procedures
    J. Escape Procedures
    K. Apprehension of Escapes
    L. Curfew Violations
    M. Procedures for Nonresident Status
    N. Overnight and Weekend Passes
    O. Critical Incidents
    P. Parole Procedures
    Q. Medical Problems
    R. Resident Record-keeping and Reporting Systems
        1. Special Reports
        2. Information Systems
        3. Staff Responsibilities
        4. Time Schedules for Records and Reporting
    S. Food Services to Residents
    T. Use, Care, and Maintenance of Vehicles
XII. Personnel Policies
XIII. Financial Management
    A. Opening and Use of Charge Accounts

B. Acquiring Supplies and Materials and/or Incurring Costs
  C. Procedures for Administering Petty Cash and/or Resident Loan Funds
XIV. Maintenance of the Physical Facility, Equipment, and Furnishings
  A. Inspections by Staff
  B. Security Procedures
  C. Furnishings Inventory
  D. Care and Maintenance of Resident Living Quarters
  E. General Building Maintenance (Interior and Exterior)
  F. Procedures for Contracting for Repairs or Maintenance of Physical Facility and Equipment
XV. Internal Office Management
  A. Office Procedures and Protocol
  B. Procedures for Handling Mail, Telephone, and Messages
  C. Supplies, Equipment, and Mailing Lists
  D. Maintenance, Distribution, and Security of Keys
  E. Typing Formats and Style
XVI. Procedure for Updating Manual
XVII. Annotated Index

Intake Procedures

It is important for purposes of evaluation and design of new approaches or modification of programs that program staff begin on the first day contact is established to collect basic information on entering residents. In addition, all information should be maintained in a file established for each resident.

There are many models of intake forms available from related social service-type programs. The two sample approaches presented here allow some measure of flexibility depending on the particular treatment modality of the project.

The first form (Figure 3-1) is an *Intake Information Form* that might be used if the staff is permitted to interview the inmate in the institution prior to release to the center. This form may be used to record information for:

1. determining eligibility for the program,
2. preliminary program planning, and
3. making preliminary community contacts relevant to the resident's program plan.

Some of the information required may be available from presentence reports, institutional classification material, or other reliable sources and should be recorded from these sources prior to the interview with the inmate. This will permit verification of information during the interview. During the initial

(Center name)
(Center address)

INTAKE INFORMATION FORM

Date of interview _____

Date of admission _____

Pretrial _____

Posttrial _____

Name _____ Interviewer _____

Identification number _____ Social Security number _____

DOB _____ Vehicle operator's permit number _____

Physical limitations (if any) _____

_____

Military service _____ Type of discharge _____

Offense or charge _____

_____

Committing judge _____ Place of conviction _____

or Court appearance _____

Sentence (state in months)

    a. Beginning _____ b. Full-term _____

    c. Short-term _____ d. Parole hearing date _____

    e. If pretrial, scheduled date of return to court

Prior criminal record _____

_____

_____

Residence prior to commitment _____

                            (City)   (County)   (State)

Family

Relationship	Name	Address	Telephone Number
Wife			
Children			
Mother			
Father			
Siblings—ages other pertinent information			
Other relatives and relevant others			

Figure 3-1. Intake Information Form

Education _____

Training _____

Employment history

Job	Employer name and address	Dates	Salary

Future employment preferences _____

Future employment leads _____

Comments _____

Brief description of apparent or stated health problems _____

Visitors while confined

Name	Address	Telephone number	Frequency of visits	Date of last visit

Figure 3-1. (cont.)

(To be completed by resident)

Name _____ Date of birth _____

Social Security Number _____

Address _____

_____

Phone number _____

What school did you attend? _____

What is the highest grade you completed in school? _____

What year did you leave school? _____

Have you been involved in a training program? If so, when and what type? _____

_____

_____

_____

Previous employment

Dates	Employer	Address	Type of business	Your job	Wages
_____	_____	_____	_____	_____	_____
_____	_____	_____	_____	_____	_____
_____	_____	_____	_____	_____	_____
_____	_____	_____	_____	_____	_____
_____	_____	_____	_____	_____	_____

Signature _____

Date _____

Figure 3-2. Résumé

interview or upon admittance to the center, each resident should also complete the "Résumé" form (Figure 3-2) that will assist in job development and placement decisions by staff and residents.

Another group of sample intake forms (Figures 3-3 to 3-5) follow that might be more appropriate for programs that receive referrals from agencies other than corrections departments and that complete the intake form at first contact with client. This basic form contains information about the client, and it is followed by a form that provides additional information about the family or others who are important to the resident.

Resident
ID Number _____

(Center Name)

(Center Address)

INTAKE FORM

1. Date _____ 2. Time _____ a.m./p.m. ☐

3. Name _____ ☐
       (Last)   (First)   (Middle)

4. Permanent address _____ ☐
       (Street)

_____ Home phone _____ ☐
    (City)   (Zip code)

5. Institution _____ ☐ _____ ☐
       Name   Date of admission

6. Birth date _____ 7. Sex: M F 8. Race/ethnic Status _____ ☐

9. Marital status _____ ☐ 10. Vehicle operator's permit number _____ ☐

11. Last grade in school completed _____ ☐ 12. Previous contacts with other agencies: Y N ☐

13. Previous contacts with police Y N ☐ 14. Previous convictions Y N ☐

15. Length of sentence _____ ☐ 16. Parole hearing date _____ ☐

17. Return to court date _____ Court _____ ☐

18. Drug-Alcohol involvement Y N 19. Military service Y N ☐

20. Employment status at time of conviction _____ ☐ 21. Social Security Number _____ ☐

22. Type of employment sought _____ ☐ 23. Expected wage rate _____ ☐

24. Religious preference _____ ☐

25. Qualitative information about family/relevant others on file Y N

26. Reported medical problems Y N ☐

27. Significant observable physical problems _____ ☐

28. Assessment of resident's interpersonal skills during interview _____ ☐

29. Disposition at first contact _____ ☐

30. Intake completed by _____ ☐

31. Counselor assigned _____ Date _____ ☐

Figure 3-3. Intake Form

The sample format of Figure 3-3 utilizes a coding system appropriate for computer processing. The form also contains "boxes" that can be checked ([x]) to indicate that additional narrative information is available in the files.

Intake Form Codes (Figure 3-3)

Resident ID Number

In the space provided at the top of the form, a code number will be assigned each resident.

```
              (Center Name)
              (Center Address)
            NARRATIVE INFORMATION
   Resident's name _____ ID Number _____
   Date _____ Person completing form _____

   Item _____ : _____
   _____
   _____

   Item _____ : _____
   _____
   _____

   Item      : _____
   _____
   _____

   Item _____ : _____
   _____
   _____

   Item _____ : _____
   _____
   _____

   Item _____ : _____
   _____
   _____

Staple this form to the form for which the narratives are provided.
```

Figure 3-4. Narrative Information

1. *Date:* Using numerals (i.e., 01/14/75) insert the date of the intake interview.
2. *Time:* Record the time of day the intake interview is completed and circle "AM" or "PM."
3. *Name:* The resident's name should be printed on the line provided. Print the last name, first name, and the middle name or middle initial, if known.
4. *Permanent address:* On the first line print the street and the house or apartment number of the resident's permanent address or that of his family. On the next line print the city or town and zip code of the permanent address. Also insert the telephone number and area code (if other than that of the center).
5. *Institution:* Insert the appropriate institution name or code number. If the center serves more than one institution, a coded list should be developed. Insert (using numerals) the date of admission of the resident to the institution noted.
6. *Birthdate:* Using numerals, insert the birthdate of the resident.
7. *Sex:* Circle whether the resident is a male or female, M for male, F for female.
8. *Race/ethnic status:* Select a code number from the list provided and indicate the race and/or ethnic status of the resident.
    (1) white
    (2) black
    (3) Spanish-surnamed
    (4) other
9. *Marital status:* This refers to the marital status of the resident. Select a code number from the list provided, and insert the appropriate number on the line provided.
    (1) married
    (2) single
    (3) divorced
    (4) separated/widowed
    (5) other
10. *Vehicle operator's permit number:* Insert the permit number of any vehicle operator's permits that are currently held and active for the resident.
11. *Last grade in school completed:* Indicate the last grade in school completed by the resident.
12. *Previous contacts with other agencies:* Circle "Y" or "N" (Y for Yes, N for No). If "yes," describe all previous agency contacts on the Narrative Form. Include agency; reason for contact; individual involved, if known; approximate date of contact; and disposition, if known.
13. *Previous contacts with police:* Circle "Y" or "N" (Y for Yes, N for No). If "yes," describe all previous contacts on the Narrative Form. Include violations, dates, and dispositions.
14. *Previous convictions:* Circle "Y" or "N" (Y for Yes, N for No). If "yes," list

this information on the Narrative Form. List any previous adjudications or incarcerations regardless of seriousness.
15. *Length of sentence:* For the present conviction, list the length of sentence. Explain on the Narrative Form any previous sentences or continuations.
16. *Parole hearing date:* If one has been established, report the parole hearing date (using numerals).
17. *Return to court date:* If the resident is in pretrial status, indicate the date (using numerals) when he must appear in court and the name and location of the court.
18. *Alcohol/drug use:* Circle "Y" or "N" (Y for Yes, N for No) for alcohol or drug involvement or problem—presently or previously. Provide an explanation on the Narrative Form.
19. *Military service:* Circle "Y" or "N" (Y for Yes, N for No) if the resident has completed military service. If "yes," explain on the Narrative Form.
20. *Employment status at time of conviction:* Select a code number from the list below and insert on the line provided. Explain details on the Narrative Form, if appropriate.
    (1) *Satisfactorily employed*: Includes residents employed full or part-time in a job with which they were satisfied.
    (2) *Not satisfactorily employed*: Includes residents employed in a job with which they were not satisfied.
    (3) *Unemployed*: Includes residents unemployed and seeking work.
    (4) *Homemakers*: Includes residents of either sex, not economically active, who were engaged in household duties in their own homes.
    (5) *Students*: Includes residents not economically active, who were attending an educational program, full or part-time.
    (6) *Other*: Includes residents not economically active who were receiving public aid or support and/or public wards.
21. *Social Security Number*: On the line provided, record the resident's social security number *from the card*—do not rely on the individual's memory.
22. *Type of employment sought:* Indicate on the line provided, the type of employment the resident is seeking, (i.e., full-time or part-time; sales, construction, etc.).
23. *Expected wage rate:* Indicate the expected salary or wage rate desired by the resident.
24. *Religious preference:* From the code list below indicate the religious preference of the resident. Residents may have few religious ties, but in those cases in which a religious preference is expressed, staff may find this an important source of supportive services for the resident.
    (01) Jewish
    (02) Catholic
    (03) Baptist
    (04) Methodist

(05) Lutheran
(06) Pentecostal
(07) Presbyterian
(08) Disciples of Christ
(09) Mohammedan
(10) Episcopal
(11) none
(12) other

25. *Qualitative information about family on file:* If additional qualitative information about the family has been provided in the file (on the Narrative Form or on other forms), so indicate by circling either "Y" (for yes) or "N" (for no).
26. *Reported medical problems:* If the resident reports any medical problems or these can be identified in files, note these on the Narrative Form and circle "Y" (for yes) or "N" (for no) for this item.
27. *Significant observable physical characteristics:* All observable, unusual physical characteristics *that are visible to the intake worker* should be noted using the codes below. Narratives, if appropriate, may be provided on the Narrative Form.
    (01) obese
    (02) underweight
    (03) several teeth missing or in need of dentures
    (04) limbs (including fingers) missing
    (05) eye irritations, unusual squinting, or eyes have unusual appearance
    (06) wears glasses
    (07) limps when walks
    (08) pregnant
    (09) uses prosthetics
    (10) physical deformities
    (11) open sores
    (12) hearing deficiency—no hearing aid
    (13) wears hearing aid
    (14) skin rashes
    (15) mental retardation
    (16) tatoos
    (17) other
28. *Assessment of resident's interpersonal relations during interview:* The intake worker should note any unusual emotional or interpersonal characteristics exhibited by the resident during the intake interview, if appropriate.
    (01) none
    (02) nervous
    (03) agitated
    (04) withdrawn/detached

(05) depressed
(06) hostile/defensive
(07) aggressive/abrasive
(08) noncommunicative
(09) suggests harm to others
(10) suggests self-destructive behavior
(11) satisfactory behavior—not able to determine any irregularities
(12) other
29. *Disposition at first contact:* Indicate, using a code number from the list below, the disposition of the case upon termination of the first interview.
   (1) plan developed
   (2) plan scheduled to be developed
   (3) family session to be scheduled
   (4) second interview scheduled
   (5) other (describe)
30. *Intake completed by:* The person completing the intake should sign his name or insert initials on the line provided.
31. *Counselor assigned:* Indicate the name of the counselor assigned this case and the date the assignment was completed.

Family Information Form Codes (Figure 3-5)

This form has been designed as an optional form to be completed for appropriate cases. The items on the form should be completed as follows:

1. *Father's name:* Print the resident's father's name on the line provided. If the name is for a guardian or foster father, provide narrative information on the Narrative Form.
2. *Age:* Provide the age of the resident's father.
3. *Father's address:* Print the street address, city or town, zip code and home phone number of the resident's father or person listed in item 1.
4. *Father's occupation:* Write the name of the father's occupation in the space provided. If the father (or person listed in item 1) is unemployed or retired, indicate his occupation and explain these circumstances on the Narrative Form.
5. *Father's level of educational attainment:* From the code list below indicate the highest level of educational attainment of the resident's father:
   (1) 8 years or less
   (2) some high school
   (3) high school graduate
   (4) technical/vocational certificate or courses completed
   (5) some college or higher education

Resident
ID Number _____

(Center Name)

(Center Address)

FAMILY INFORMATION

1. Father's name _____ ☐   2. Age _____ ☐
3. Father's address _____ ☐
   _____ Phone _____ ☐

   Father's   Father's level of
4. Occupation _____ ☐   5. educational attainment _____ ☐
6. Father's employer _____ ☐   Phone _____ ☐
7. Mother's name _____ ☐   8. Age _____ ☐
9. Mother's address _____ ☐
   _____ Phone _____ ☐

   Mother's   Mother's level of
10. occupation _____ ☐   11. educational attainment _____ ☐
12. Mother's employer _____ ☐   Phone _____ ☐
13. Marital status of parents _____ ☐
14. Siblings   ☐

First name	Age	Address

15. Medical problems of relatives?   Y   N   ☐
16. Relevant others _____
_____

17. Religious preference of family _____ ☐
18. Annual gross family income _____ ☐
19. Information completed by _____ Date _____

Figure 3-5. Family Information

(6) 4 years of college
(7) 5 or more years of college
6. *Father's employer:* If employed, in the space provided, indicate the name and phone number of the father's employer, company, or immediate supervisor at his job.
7. *Mother's name:* Print the resident's mother's name on the line provided. If the name is for a guardian or foster mother, provide narrative information on the Narrative Form.
8. *Age:* Provide the age of the resident's mother.
9. *Mother's address:* Print the street address, city or town, zip code, and home phone number of the resident's mother or person listed in item 7.
10. *Mother's occupation:* Write the name of the mother's occupation in the space provided. If the mother (or person listed in item 7) is unemployed, retired, or a housewife, indicate any occupation for which she is trained and explain these circumstances on the Narrative Form.
11. *Mother's level of educational attainment:* From the code list below, indicate the highest level of educational attainment of the resident's mother.
    (1) 8 years or less
    (2) some high school
    (3) high school graduate
    (4) technical/vocational certificate or courses completed
    (5) some college or higher education
    (6) 4 years of college
    (7) 5 or more years of college
12. *Mother's employer:* If employed, in the space provided, indicate the name and phone number of the mother's employer, company, and immediate supervisor at her job.
13. *Marital status of parents:* List here the marital status of the resident's parents or foster parents (indicate information for resident's present family if not natural parents), by selecting a code number from the list below and inserting it on the line provided.
    (1) married, living together
    (2) separated
    (3) divorced
    (4) unwed mother
    (5) unwed father
    (6) reconstituted family (one natural parent, one stepparent)
    (7) other
14. *Siblings:* Print the first name of each sibling of the resident and the age and address of each.
15. *Medical problems of relatives:* Indicate medical problems of relatives known to resident on the Narrative Form. In this space circle "Y" (for yes) or "N" (for no), indicating if problems were reported.

16. *Relevant others:* List here the name, relationship, address, and phone number of any relevant others noted in files or during discussions with the resident. This might include friends, religious workers, frequent visitors, employers, etc.
17. *Religious preference of family:* Indicate here the religious preference of the family by selecting a code number from the list below and placing it on the line provided.
    (01) Jewish
    (02) Catholic
    (03) Baptist
    (04) Methodist
    (05) Lutheran
    (06) Pentecostal
    (07) Presbyterian
    (08) Disciples of Christ
    (09) Mohammedan
    (10) Episcopal
    (11) none
    (12) other
18. *Annual gross family income:* Select from the list provided the approximate income level of the resident's immediate family and record the appropriate code number in the space provided.
    (01) Welfare, AFDC
    (02) Less than $2,500
    (03) $2,501-$7,500
    (04) $7,501-$10,000
    (05) $10,001-$15,000
    (06) $15,001-$20,000
    (07) $20,001-$25,000
    (08) $25,001-$30,000
    (09) $30,001-$35,000
    (10) More than $35,000
19. *Information completed by:* The staff member recording information on this form should sign the form or insert initials on the line provided. The date the form is completed should also be recorded.

Program Plan

A program plan should be developed for each resident. This may be in the form of a narrative contractual agreement between the resident and the staff, or it may be a form that specifies objectives and goals and that places responsibility for each on residents as well as staff. Samples of these two approaches follow

(Figures 3-6 to 3-9). An assessment plan for noting progress on a regular basis must be developed. This might be recorded on the form itself, provided separately through staff reviews, or generated by the information system (see Chapter 4).

Parole Procedures and Forms

Some residents who are still under sentence may arrive at the center with an assigned parole hearing date, and others may receive hearing date assignments while in the center. Prior to the parole hearing, staff will probably be required to submit a parole plan for each resident to the appropriate Parole Board. Steps in this process and suggested forms to be used are presented here:

1. *Submission of parole plan:* The first form (Figure 3-10) may be used to submit a resident's parole plan and to request evaluation of the proposed plan by the appropriate parole authority who would then notify the center of whether the plan is approved. This form should be initiated at least two weeks in advance of the parole date and, if warranted, in advance of the parole hearing. A copy of the current Parole Progress Report (see item 3 and Figure 3-13) should accompany the request.
2. *Notification of resident population of parole hearing date:* The next two forms (Figures 3-11 and 3-12) should be used to notify residents and nonresidents of their parole hearings. A memorandum is sufficient for those in resident status. This should be delivered by the resident's counselor or other designated staff. For those in nonresident status, a certified letter with a return receipt should be required. Copies of both notifications should be retained in the resident's Center file.
3. *Parole progress report:* A suggested format for parole progress reports is presented in Figure 3-13. It is important that a standard format be used. The report presents a written record about the resident to be submitted to the parole authority at the time of a parole hearing. A copy of this report should be provided to the assigned parole and probation officer along with the request for parole plan evaluation discussed in item 1 above.

Follow-up

Follow-up contacts should occur with all residents who have received services from the center; a regular follow-up should be completed at the three-month and six-month dates following termination of residents from the center (including those paroled, rearrested, or returned to institutions). This information will assist the evaluator in determining the degree of program and individual client success or failure. It will also provide data for comparative studies, cost-benefit analyses, recidivism studies, cohort analysis studies of terminated residents, etc.

(Center Name)

(Center Address)

PROGRAM PRESCRIPTION RECORD

Resident _____   Resident ID _____

Target area	Activities planned	Progress (o=UNSAT; +=SAT) Months												
		J	F	M	A	M	J	J	A	S	O	N	D
Economic status	Plan												
	Modifications												
Family conditions	Plan												
	Modifications												
Mental health	Plan												
	Modifications												
Physical health	Plan												
	Modifications												
Education	Plan												
	Modifications												
Job training	Plan												
	Modifications												
Social skills	Plan												
	Modifications												
Special problem area	Plan												
	Modifications												

Prepared by _____ Date _____

Figure 3-6. Program Prescription Record

(Name of Center)
(Center Address)

RESIDENT PLAN

Page ____ of ____

Date plan initiated ________
Date plan amended ________
Amendment number ________

Name ________ Resident ID number ________ Staff person assisting in development of plan ________

Areas of Concern	Objectives	How objectives will be achieved	Target date	Resident responsibilities	Staff responsibilities	Family/others responsibilities	Comments

Figure 3-7. Resident Plan

Agreement
Between
(Name of Resident)
and
(Name of Center)
(Address of Center)

The main emphasis of the _____ program is effective career development of its residents. Residents of _____ are required to develop a career plan with Center staff before arrival.

How successfully you and the staff follow your Career Plan will determine many of the privileges and freedoms extended to you during your residence, and even your eventual parole date.

Attached to and made a part of this Agreement is a copy of your Career Plan, the rules, regulations, and privileges of the Center, and material stating program policies and procedures.

1. I, _____, have read, discussed, and understand the policies and procedures and the rules and regulations of this Center. I agree to follow these rules, regulations, and program policies.
2. I agree to put forth my best effort for my own personal progress and development, and I agree to work at all times toward the improvement of this Center for the good of myself and all the other residents who come here.
3. I agree to follow the Career Plan that I have developed with the Center staff, and:

   a. the staff will guarantee me a minimum of two job possibilities and/or training or school programs useful to my vocational objective not later than the last day of the first week of my residence at the center;
   b. I agree to accept, if offered, one of these job placements and/or training/education as called for in my Career Plan;
   c. If I refuse a job/training opening offered to me, or if I quit my job/training without valid reason as determined by Center staff, I understand that I must obtain suitable employment within seven days; I understand that failure to do so may result in return to confinement;
   d. I agree to work with staff in seeking better employment during my residence that may be a job paying a higher wage or an advancement;
   e. I agree to accept, if offered, a better job opportunity; and
   f. if I have not completed high school or obtained my GED certificate, I understand that I will be required to enroll in GED classes or tutoring.

4. I will meet regularly with staff to work on my Career Plan, to discuss accomplishment of my goals, and to review and discuss my performance as a resident of this Center.
5. Center staff agree to be available 24 hours per day for consultation. Requests for consultation with a specific staff member can be scheduled.
6. Staff agree to provide me reasonable assistance with family and personal problems as they affect my current plans and needs and to help me identify other sources of help.
7. This Center will provide me a clean and attractive place to live and nutritious meals without cost until I have been employed for _____days, after which I understand and agree that I shall pay a subsistance allowance of $ _____ per day promptly upon receipt of my paychecks for as long as I reside in the Center.

Figure 3-8. Agreement

8. I understand that I must deposit in a savings account 5 percent of the gross amount of each paycheck I receive beginning with receipt of the first pay.
9. The center agrees to provide public transportation funds for me for _____ days prior to employment and/or until I receive my first paycheck.
10. If my progress toward my career objective and if my performance in abiding by the rules and regulations of the Center are satisfactory as determined by Center staff, the staff is obligated to recommend me for parole no later than _____.
11. If progress on my Career Plan is deemed by Center staff to be unsatisfactory, or if I fail to follow satisfactorily the Center rules and regulations, I understand that parole will not be recommended and that I may be returned to confinement.

Date _____   Resident _____

Date _____   Counselor _____

Figure 3-8. (cont.)

The importance of follow-up data and information cannot be noted too emphatically here. The two sample forms in Figures 3-14 and 3-15 might serve as appropriate guides.

(Center Name)
(Center Address)

CAREER PLAN

For (name) _____ ID Number _____

Vocational objectives
    Primary _____
    Secondary _____

Educational objectives _____

	Type/course	Expected completion date
Training necessary 1.	_____	_____
2.	_____	_____
3.	_____	_____

	Name	Location
Training resources 1.	_____	_____
2.	_____	_____
3.	_____	_____

Entry-level job identified
(Use job titles here, not employers)
    Stage I _____
    Stage II _____
    Stage III _____

Estimated time required to realize stated objective _____

What activities are necessary by the staff career developer?
1. _____
2. _____
3. _____
4. _____

The career advisor or counselor shall assume responsibility to plan with the resident his career objective and to provide those resources, contacts, and support necessary to obtain realistic objectives in the shortest time possible.

Counselor _____ Date _____ Resident _____ Date _____

Figure 3-9. Career Plan

PAROLE PLAN FORM LETTER
(Center Name)
(Center Address)

Date _____

To _____
    (Parole and Probation Officer)
    (address)

                                        RE:
                                        ID No.:

Dear Sir:
    The above named resident has a tentative parole date of _____
_____.

The following parole program is proposed

Residence

Employment

    Please return one copy of this letter advising if this parole program is acceptable to your office for supervision.

                                Sincerely,

                                Director

The above release program is approved for parole supervision.

                                Approved

_____   _____
Parole Officer   Supervisor

(Use reverse side for comments.)

Figure 3-10. Parole Plan Form Letter

(For use with residents)
(Name and address of Center)

NOTIFICATION OF PAROLE HEARING: RESIDENTS

MEMORANDUM

To _____ Date _____
From _____, Center director _____
Subject: Parole hearing

    You are scheduled to appear before the parole board at

        Time _____
        Day _____
        Date _____
        Place _____

Please plan to be present before the meeting is scheduled to begin.

Memo received _____ Date _____

Distribution: Original to resident
                    Signed copy to center file
                    Signed copy to institution file
                    Counselor

Figure 3-11. Notification of Parole Hearing: Residents

(For use with nonresidents)
(Name, address, and telephone number of Center)

NOTIFICATION OF PAROLE HEARING: NONRESIDENTS

Date _____

Certified Mail—Return Receipt Requested

Dear _____ :

The Parole Board has scheduled a meeting to consider granting you parole. *You are required to be at the meeting.* It is scheduled for:

Time _____
Day _____
Date _____
Place _____

Please plan to arrive before the meeting is scheduled to start.

Sincerely,

Center Director

cc: Counselor
　　Center file
　　Institution file

Figure 3-12. Notification of Parole Hearing: Nonresidents

(Name and Address of Center)

PAROLE PROGRESS REPORT

Date _____

Name _____ ID number _____
Offense _____ Age _____
Sentence _____ Began _____ Months served _____
Last board action and date _____
Sentence expires _____

Current offense

Official account: A description of the offense, including loss to victim.

Offender's explanation: A current summary of the offender's explanation and attitude regarding the offense.

Codefendants: Provide significant and available information, including names, sentencing data, present location, and current status, if known.

Committed Name   ID Number   Date

Background

Prior record: In two or three sentences, summarize briefly the offender's experience with the criminal justice system, i.e., age at first arrest, number of arrests and convictions, types of offenses, and any new information not previously available.

Detainers: Current status of all pending charges and detainers.

Past history: A brief summary of significant information related to the offender, such as social history, education, military experience, and employment. This paragraph should also include any information not previously available.

Figure 3-13. Parole Progress Report

Institutional and community progress

Goals: Summarize goals established, goals completed, and progress toward remaining goals, with special emphasis on goals established and progress since arrival at the Center.

Institutional adjustment: Evaluate the offender's response to institutional experience, i.e., conduct, work assignments, leisure time, and obvious changes in character traits.

Physical and mental health: Indicate the status of the offender's current mental and physical health, including a comment regarding employability. Separate psychiatric or psychological reports may be attached to the Progress Report.

Release resources and plans

Prerelease resources: Summary of current or anticipated involvement in prerelease programming, i.e., work release, Community Treatment Center, study release, furloughs, town trips.

Postrelease resources: Statement of verified resources available for the offender after release, i.e., family, private agencies, community programs, savings, employment placement officer, and others.

Postcommitment plans:

A. Residence—address and relationship to the offender.

B. Employer—name and address of employer, job, and wages.

Evaluation of release readiness

Probable community adjustment: Evaluation of offender's ability to remain in the community without violating the law.

Recommendation: A statement of recommendation for or against granting the parole. If the recommendation is negative, this paragraph should also include a comment regarding future parole review. If the recommendation is positive, summarize postcommitment treatment needs and suggested program involvement. In a few instances, it may be necessary to explain different staff opinion regarding a recommendation, and in special situations, it may not be advisable to make a recommendation at all.

Figure 3-13. (cont.)

(Center Name)
(Center Address)

FOLLOW-UP CONTACT FORM

Date _____ Time _____ Staff person completing contact _____
Name _____ Resident ID number _____
Type of follow-up _____ Place of contact _____ ☐
Others present (list names and relationship to resident) _____
_____ ☐

Reason for follow-up
Former resident is participating in educational activities at present?   Y   N   ☐
Former resident is receiving services from other agencies at present?   Y   N   ☐
Former resident is employed at present?   Y   N   ☐
Recommendations _____
_____
_____

Next suggested follow-up contact _____

Update information
Resident's marital status _____ ☐   Resident's job status _____ ☐
Job title _____ ☐   Work phone _____
Employer _____ ☐   Phone _____
Name change _____ ☐
Date of job change _____ ☐   School status _____ ☐
Other information _____
_____
_____
_____ ☐

(Codes may be developed for this form, or information may be recorded on the form.)
[X] Narrative information on file.

Figure 3-14. Follow-up Contact Form

(Center Name)

(Center Address)

FOLLOW-UP REPORT FORM

Resident _____ ID Number _____

Release date _____ Type of release _____

Status	Three months (circle one)	Six months (circle one)
Employed	Yes No	Yes No
Same job	Yes No	Yes No
Same family situation	Yes No	Yes No
Arrest-free	Yes No	Yes No
Conviction-free	Yes No	Yes No
Wages	$ /week	$ /week

Services requested	Three months			Six months		
	Provided	Successful	Dollar cost	Provided	Successful	Dollar cost
Job placement	Yes No	Yes No	$	Yes No	Yes No	$
Counseling	Yes No	Yes No	$	Yes No	Yes No	$
Legal	Yes No	Yes No	$	Yes No	Yes No	$
Education/training	Yes No	Yes No	$	Yes No	Yes No	$
Health	Yes No	Yes No	$	Yes No	Yes No	$

Source of information _____

Services provided by _____

Report prepared by _____
                              Name

_____   _____
          Title   Date

Figure 3-15. Follow-up Report Form

4 The Management Information System (MIS)

Introduction

A Management Information System (MIS) is a valuable tool for providing not only comprehensive information to staff for ongoing evaluation of direct services and client progress, but it is also useful in developing long-range plans and determining client success. It is an organized method of collecting and recording information about the operation of a program.

An MIS was developed and refined by SERD for The SERD/Congress Heights Human Development Center (SERD/CHHDC) to provide daily, weekly, monthly, quarterly, and annually detailed information about residents and program activity. The primary objective of the system was to provide an overall assessment and picture of residents individually and collectively, to assess progress, and to identify and anticipate problems before they arose. The system provided a tool for administrative and management staff to evaluate and modify the total program and to measure staff accountability.

The MIS could be adapted easily to any similar program. At SERD/CHHDC it was the most important record-keeping system as it provided a data base for all areas of evaluation. The effectiveness of the system depends on each individual staff member's commitment to recording accurate data on a regular schedule. Data from the MIS Report Form were cumulated and recorded on MIS Summary Forms weekly, monthly, quarterly, and annually. The MIS Report and Summary Forms are included in this section.

Goals and Objectives

The MIS developed by SERD/CHHDC provided daily, weekly, and monthly detailed information about residents. The primary objective of the system was to provide an overall assessment and picture of the residents individually and collectively to identify and anticipate problems before they arose. The system also was a tool for administrative and management staff to evaluate and modify the total SERD/CHHDC program.

If the information required is reported regularly, the system should provide the following specific information to caseworkers and counselors:

1. information about the resident's daily activities,

2. a brief but overall picture of the resident's present and past program status,
3. progress made by the resident,
4. any behavior problems,
5. the relationships between and among activities, progress, and behavior, and
6. a guide for comparison with other residents in the Center.

The administrative staff of the Center used the system to identify potential "Intensive Care"[a] residents, to provide follow-up between counselors and the residents, and to identify program successes and deficiencies.

For the system to be effective, it must be used regularly by all staff, and it should be modified regularly to cope with new problems and requirements. The process is circular, and if any step is skipped or ignored, the cycle will be broken.

The MIS Report Form

Structure of the Form

The MIS Report Form is structured to provide entries for each resident for one month. It is a simple checklist; items are listed in the column on the left-hand side of the sheet with blocks for entries to the right of each item. The form contains five weekly cells with daily designations in each cell plus one weekly column. Toward the top and to the left is a space for the month. Directly below the month are spaces for the resident's name and date of the first contact with the resident. To the right is a space for the name of the staff member making the entries. The reverse side of the form should be used for comments.

Where to Make Entries

All entries are to be made in the block that corresponds to the correct date of the month and day of the week. There is one extra block at the end of each week (marked "W"). This space should be used to record weekly entries only. The final item (M2–Points Accumulated in CAP) has designated space to enter the number of points accumulated by a resident that week in the Credit Advancement Program (CAP).

How to Make Entries

An entry is an "x" made in a designated block directly to the right of an item. For daily items a slash (/) must be made in each block to indicate that this item

---

[a]"Intensive Care" residents are residents with whom the staff are having difficulty formulating plans that move the residents successfully through the program. The residents are then given "intensive attention" by the staff to identify a viable course of action.

was checked. If upon checking, the item has occurred, then the entry should be an "x."

When making entries in the weekly section, the entry "x" should be made in the block that corresponds to the day of the week the action occurred and the number of occurrences of that item that week should be entered in the "W" column.

Entries that require a report to be on file are marked with an asterisk. If the staff member reporting took any specific action on the problem or item identified, the "x" should be circled—ⓧ. The action taken should be explained on the back of the form in the "comments" section or if required, in a detailed report on file. Reports in the Center resident's file should appear on a *Critical Incident Report* form or on a *Contact Form*.

If the situation requires that the entry reflect more than one occurrence of an item in one day, the entry should be modified by adding a vertical mark "ᚷ". (It is very important that all entries be confined to their designated space to prevent confusion with others.)

When to Make Entries

Forms for each resident were maintained at the Center with entries made daily, weekly, and as events occurred in the life of the resident. The items are divided into three categories.

1. *Daily entries:* The first group of items were checked daily (by midnight) without fail and the appropriate marks recorded in each block.
2. *Weekly entries:* The second group of items were checked weekly and appropriate marks recorded each Friday in the "W" column.
3. *Entries to be checked when necessary:* The last group of items reflect actions that were not "scheduled" and were marked whenever the action occurred.

Coding Formula

The structure of the code is very simple; the alphabet designates areas of vital information and the numbers specify items within that area. The alphabetical code is as follows.

A   resident motivation and overall plan and adjustment
C   counseling
D   drugs
E   education or training
F   family involvement
J   job or employment information
M   miscellaneous
P   problem areas

Whenever feasible the alphabetical letters correspond to the first letter of the area of information. The numbers do not necessarily reflect a sequence but were used merely to identify items within a particular area. It is very important that particularly close attention be paid to the abbreviations used. They are explained in more detail later.

What Entries to Make

Each designation should be read thoroughly before making an entry. The items listed for daily consideration should become a matter of routine. Those items in the category of "whenever necessary" are very important to aid in reporting successes and achievements and problem identification. They must be reviewed daily in an effort to leave no actions unrecorded.

Items that required a report be placed on file in the resident's center file are followed by an asterisk (*). This report was usually recorded on the Critical Incident Report or other appropriate form. The reports contained the following information:

1. a review of the facts and circumstances leading up to the incident,
2. a complete factual account of the incident,
3. involvement by Center staff, Department of Corrections personnel, family, and others during the incident,
4. disposition and/or staff recommendation, and
5. a plan for preventing future occurrences.

All reports were on file within 24 hours of the incident.

Abbreviations used on the MIS Report Form include:

R   Resident
Cr   Counselor
CS   Counseling session
CAS   Credit Advancement System (or Program)
NTA   Narcotic Treatment Administration Program
U/S   Urine Sample
Comm. Projects   Community Projects
S/TP   School/Training Program
I/P   Increase/Promotion
IC   Intensive Care

A detailed explanation of each item on the form follows.

(*DAILY:* Daily items were checked daily and a slash (/) entered in the space opposite each item. If the item applied to the resident that day, the entry was an "x.")

Code	Designation	Use
C1	CS initiated by R*	In any instance when a resident requests a counseling session with his counselor, an entry "x" should be made opposite this item. The item should be considered daily, including Saturday and Sunday if applicable. A "session" is defined as a meeting called to impart or receive information. If the session is related to one of the subsequently listed problem areas, the entry should be circled and a brief but concise narrative report placed in the files. If the session is not related to a listed problem area, the entry must be made in the proper space, and a short statement relating to the essence of the session must be entered in the "comment" section on the back of the form. While there is no time limit established for a "session," a simple telephone contact initiated by the resident with his counselor will not, except in the most unusual circumstances, be considered a counseling session initiated by the resident.
C5	R had individual CS as scheduled	Every resident, whether on in-count or out-count status, is expected to have at least one scheduled individual (i.e., private) counseling session with his counselor each week. Some residents will have more than one scheduled session per week. The counselor will make an entry "x" opposite this item whenever a resident attends a scheduled session.
D2	Failed to report to NTA	If the resident has been referred to a Narcotics Treatment Administration (NTA) Program and upon checking, it is revealed that he did not keep his appointment, an entry "x" should be made opposite this item.
D3	U/S not collected as scheduled	On any occasion when a resident has been scheduled to produce a urine specimen and fails to do so, an entry "x" should be made opposite this item.
J2	R is unemployed	This entry should reflect the daily employment status of a resident. Unemployed residents will be identified with an "x."
J3	R had job interview today	On any day when a resident reports to an employer for a job or school interview, an entry "x" should be made opposite this item. The resident's counselor is responsi-

Code	Designation	Use
		ble for the entry but should make such entry only on proof of interview, such as a completed job interview sheet returned by the resident or verification by the counselor with the prospective employer or school official.
J4	Employer follow-up by Cr*	An entry "x" should be made opposite this item whenever an employment follow-up or visit is made by the counselor or caseworker. If the visit produces any information that may reflect the type of adjustment or the attitude of the resident, an explanation should be made in the comment section on the back of the form.
P6	R violated curfew	On any day when the resident returns more than 15 minutes late for curfew, an "x" should be made opposite this item.

(WEEKLY: An "x" should be made in the space opposite each item indicating the day an incident occurred unless otherwise specified. The total number of entries "x" opposite each item for the week should be entered in the "W" column unless otherwise specified.)

Code	Designation	Use
A1	Resident motivation	Residents should not be rated on this item until they have lived in the Center for two full weeks. This item should be considered each Friday, and a number ranging from 1 through 5 should be entered in the "W" column. The counselor or caseworker should consider the resident's activities during the past week and rate him on the following scale. 1. This resident shows very little or no motivation, interest, or personal growth. He is unemployed, breaks rules, violates curfew, most likely has drug problems, does not help with work around the Center, misses meals, and refuses to get up in the morning. 2. This resident shows some signs of motivation, but demonstrates little initiative in dealing with his problems. There is evidence that he has been using drugs

Code	Designation	Use

      in the past month. He has been employed in one or more jobs that he has quit with no reasonable explanation. He has no career plan but is somewhat articulate about his personal problems.

3. This resident seems to move forward and backward in terms of motivation. He has had several positive urine samples. He is indecisive about his career and/or personal problems.
4. This resident demonstrates positive signs of motivation and has a fairly good understanding of his own problems. He may have had one positive urine during the past month. He has a job or is enrolled full-time in school or a training program. He has been reasonably attentive to his job or school—only missing one or two days per month. However, his job has no growth potential and does not motivate him toward any higher career aspirations. His grades in school are average or slightly above. He is prompt and reliable in terms of Center activities and rules.
5. This resident has a high degree of self-motivation and a very good understanding of his own problems. He has no drug problems and has been free for at least one full month or more. He is employed full-time or pursuing a realistic career plan with a realistic goal in view. He relates well to staff and other residents, abides by rules, and has a realistic conception of himself.

A2   Resident contract   This item refers to the contract between SERD/CHHDC and each resident that was established before the resident arrives at SERD/CHHDC. A number entry should be inserted weekly in the "W" column to indicate status and progress of the contract. The entry number should be selected from the following:

1. contract proposed,
2. contract accepted by both parties,
3. resident progressing as specified in contract,
4. resident progress not related to contract,
5. contract modified, or
6. little or no progress toward contract by resident to date.

Code	Designation	Use
		The resident's counselor is responsible for this weekly entry and establishing the rating used. Whenever a rating of 4, 5, or 6 is used by a counselor, a brief explanation for use of this particular rating is to be made on the back of the MIS Report Form.
A3	IC status of R	This item should be marked with a number entry from the following list at the end of each week in the "W" column. This item refers only to residents in Intensive Care (IC). For all other residents, a slash (/) should be inserted in the "W" column. 1. R placed in Intensive Care with written prescription. 2. R in Intensive Care making progress toward completing prescription. 3. R has successfully completed prescription and has been removed from Intensive Care. 4. R is not making progress. 5. Deadline for achieving prescription passed, and R did not achieve; prescription modified first time. 6. Deadline for achieving prescription passed, and R did not achieve; prescription modified second time. 7. Deadline for achieving prescription passed, and R did not achieve; prescription modified three times or more.
C2	Contact by Department of Corrections staff, C&P officers, etc.*	An entry "x" should be made in the space opposite this item each time contact occurs between the C&P Officer or other Department of Corrections official. The weekly total should be entered in the "W" column. A brief explanation of who made the contact and why should be made on the back of the MIS Report Form by the staff person contacted.
C3	R attended group CS	An entry "x" in the space opposite this item will record resident attendance at scheduled group or Center meetings. The weekly total should be entered in the "W" column.
D1	Positive urine	The entry in the space opposite this item should be on the date a positive specimen was collected. For example, if the sample was collected on August 25, the entry

Code	Designation	Use
		should correspond to that date on the form. The Chief House Supervisor will be the only person to record positive urine samples on individual MIS Report Forms. For all positive urine samples so reported, a brief explanation on the back of the MIS shall be made, e.g., "June 16, Quinine/Morphine."[b]
F3	Family CS with R's family*	An entry "x" should be made each time the counselor or caseworker meets with the resident's family. A report of this session must be on file.
J8	R earning $2/hr or above	An entry "x" is made opposite this item in the "W" column each appropriate week to indicate that the resident's salary rate is $2/hour or above.
J9	R received and reported wages	An entry "x" opposite this item signifies that the resident recorded his wages at the Center as required.
M2	Number of credits accumulated in CAP	The number of credits earned by the resident in the Credit Advancement Program for the week should be entered opposite this item the Monday following credit earnings.

(*CHECK WHEN NECESSARY:* As required, an entry should be made opposite the items in this group.)

Code	Designation	Use
C4	Job CS with R	In any instance when resident is counseled concerning a job related problem, i.e., lateness to work, unauthorized absence, disruptive conduct on job, loafing, etc.; an "x" should be made opposite this item.
D4	R referred to NTA*	To signify date of referral to a Narcotic Treatment Administration program, an "x" should be made opposite this item.

---

[b]The recording and tracking of drug use was based on heroin and methadone usage because in the mid-1970's, these drugs were the most seriously used drugs by the kinds of clients served in the SERD/CHHDC program.

Code	Designation	Use
E2	R received GED/other certificate/ education stipend*	To signify the date of graduation, completion of a course or training program, or to indicate receipt of an educational stipend, an "x" should be entered opposite this item.
F1	R's family requested assistance from Center staff	When a resident's family initiates a request for assistance with a problem related to the resident, an "x" should be entered in the space opposite this item. An explanation must be provided on the back of the form.
F4	Family problem identified*	When a problem is identified that relates to the family environment, i.e., marital problems, family rejection or pressure, overprotection, etc., an "x" should be entered in the space opposite this item.
J7	R received salary I/P	If a resident receives a salary increase or job promotion, an "x" must be entered in the space opposite this item. A comment should be entered on the back of the form.
M3	R developed/ reviewed budget with Cr	At the time a resident develops a budget and/or reviews it with his counselor/caseworker, an "x" should be entered in the space opposite this item. A copy of the budget and a report of the review session should be placed in the resident's file.
P1	R restricted to Center*	If a resident is restricted to the Center for any amount of time, an "x" should be entered in the space opposite this item. If the restriction is for more than one day, an "x" should be entered each day. A report must be in the resident's file.
P2	Behavior problem identified*	An "x" should be entered in the space opposite this item in any instance when a behavioral problem of the resident is identified. The problem itself may have psychological, financial, drug-related, social, or family connected roots. Any behavioral problem which, in the counselor's view, is retarding the resident's development toward out-count and eventual parole should be explained in a special report in the resident's file.

Code	Designation	Use
P3	Police contact involving R*	An "x" opposite this item records any contact with the police involving the resident, i.e., traffic tickets, questioning on new offenses or old offenses, appearance in court by subpoena, etc. A report must be in the resident's file.
P4	Medical problem involving R*	If a resident is referred to a clinic or doctor, an "x" should be entered in the space opposite this item. A report of the incident must be in the resident's file.
P7	R failed to report in	All residents of the Center including those on out-count are required to be physically at the Center or to report to the Center by telephone between the hours of 4:00 p.m. and 7:00 p.m. each day of the week. An "x" should be entered opposite this item for each daily failure to so report. This entry should be made only by the 2:00 p.m. to 10:00 p.m. supervisor.
P10	R arrested/ apprehended*	If a resident is arrested by the police, an "x" must be entered in the space opposite this item. A report must be on file. A resident who has been placed on escape from the Center and is subsequently apprehended by the police must have an apprehension report filed with the DCDC Director of Youth Services relative to his apprehension. A copy of this report must be filed in the resident's house file.
P11	R returned to custody*	If a resident is returned to the Lorton Youth Center or the D.C. Jail by SERD/CHHDC, an "x" should be entered in the space opposite this item.
P12	R placed on escape*	An "x" should be entered in the space opposite this item for the appropriate date that the resident has been officially placed in escape status by the Center. A detailed report is required both for the resident's Center file and for the DCDC Director of Youth Services. This report should be prepared by the appropriate counselor and transmitted through the Chief of Programs.

Code	Designation	Use
R1	R's parole hearing scheduled	When a parole hearing is scheduled for the resident, the date of the hearing should be entered in the appropriate space opposite this item.
R2	R's parole approved	An entry "x" in the space opposite this item designates the date of parole approval for R. Effective date of the parole should be noted on the back of the form..
R3	R's parole denied or postponed*	An entry "x" in the space opposite this item designates the date of parole denial or postponement. A report must be on file.

The back of the MIS Report Form should be used for comments as indicated previously. The code number should be included for each item preceding the comments referring to that item. The MIS Report Form follows (Figure 4-1).

MIS Summary Forms

A staff member checked all MIS Report Forms daily to be sure counselors were keeping information current. Weekly the Chief of Operations transferred data from the individual MIS Report Forms for each resident to the Weekly Summary Forms for the week ending the previous Sunday night. This information was reproduced and made available to all staff, SERD, the Department of Corrections and other authorized personnel (as determined by the Director of SERD/CHHDC) by the following Wednesday evening. Monthly, quarterly, and annual summaries were also compiled for use by staff and others.

One additional item contained on the Summary Forms was the overall resident-assessment scale. This scale identifies all residents of the Center by their overall progress in the program. The placement of a resident on the scale is determined by the number of points accumulated by tallying the information on the MIS Report Form according to numerical weights assigned each item. In the far right column on the form, numbers in parentheses (which should be developed for each program) identify the points assigned each item. The total number of points accumulated each week identify the resident's position on the scale. The scale ranges from one through ten. Residents falling in the category of 3 or below on the scale may be potential problems or need assistance. Residents in the category of 4 through 6 are probably adjusting and progressing through the program but should be watched carefully by their counselor. Residents in the range from 7 through 10 are probably well adjusted and self-motivated, are receiving maximum benefits from the program, the staff and the community, and are well on their way toward achieving their personal goals. Copies of the Summary Forms follow (Figures 4-2 to 4-5).

63

_____ (Month)

_____ (Resident)

_____ (Date of 1st Contact w/R)

SERD/Congress Heights Human Development Center
406 Condon Terrace, S.E.
Washington, D.C. 20032

_____ (Counselor)

☐ In-Count
☐ Out-Count

DAILY:

Code	Designation	
C1	CS initiated by R*	C
C5	R had indiv. CS as scheduled	C
D2	Failed to report to N.T.A.	C
D3	U/S not collected as scheduled	S
J2	R is unemployed	C
J3	R had job interview today	C
J4	Employer follow-up by Cr*	C
P6	R violated curfew	S

WEEKLY:

Code	Designation	
A1	Resident Motivation	C
A2	Resident contract	C
A3	IC status of R	C
C2	Contact by Corrections Dept., staff, C&P Officer *	C
C3	R attended group CS	C
D1	Positive Urine (report sample date)	C
F3	Family CS with R's family*	C
J8	R earning $2/hr or above	C
J9	R received and reported wages	C
M2	Number of points accumulated in CAP	C

Figure 4-1. MIS Report Form

CHECK WHEN NECESSARY:

Code	Designation		M T W T F S S W M T W T F S S W M T W T F S S W M T W T F S S W
C4	Job CS with R	C	
D4	R referred to N.T.A. today*	C	
E2	R received GED/other certificate/educa. stipend*	C	
F1	R's family requested assistance from CHHDC staff*	C	
F4	Family problem identified*	C	
J7	R received salary i/p	C	
M3	R developed/reviewed budget w/CR	C	
P1	R restricted to Center*	S	
P2	Behavior problem of R identified*	C	
P3	Police contact involving R*	C	
P4	Medical problem involving R*	S&C	
P7	R failed to report in	S	
P10	R arrested/apprehended*	C	
P11	R's returned to Custody*	CP	
P12	R placed on escape*	CP	
R1	R's parole hearing scheduled	CP	
R2	R's parole approved	CP	
R3	R's parole denied or postponed*		

* Report should be on File

Figure 4-1. (cont.)

SERD/Congress Heights Human Development Center
406 Condon Terrace, S.E.
Washington, D.C. 20032

MIS WEEKLY SUMMARY FORM

No. residents _____ No. residents in intensive care _____ (Identify with an asterisk beside name.)

Name of resident	Report number of entries for week for each item.											Report number entered for each item.							Resident assessment scale	
	D3	J2	P6	DI	P1	P2	P3	P4	P7	P10	R3	Couns.	A1	A2	A3	B1	B2	C2	M2	Total points	Position

Figure 4-2. MIS Weekly Summary Form

Month _____

SERD/Congress Heights Human Development Center
406 Condon Terrace, S.E.
Washington, D.C. 20032

MIS MONTHLY SUMMARY FORM

No. residents at beginning of month _____ No. residents at end of month _____

	Item	Number residents
D3	U/S not collected as scheduled 3 times or more	
J2	Unemployed more than 5 days	
P6	Violated curfew more than once/week	
D1	More than 1 positive urine	
P1	Restricted to the Center 1 or more times	
P2	Behavior problems identified	
P3	Police contact	
P4	Medical problem	
P10	Arrested	
R3	Parole denied or postponed	
A3	Residents in Intensive Care	

Resident Assessment Scale

Position	1	2	3	4	5	6	7	8	9	10
No. residents										

Figure 4-3. MIS Monthly Summary Form

Quarter

SERD/Congress Heights Human Development Center

406 Condon Terrace, S.E.

Washington, D.C. 20032

MIS QUARTERLY SUMMARY FORM

No. residents at beginning quarter _____ No. residents at end of quarter _____

Item		Number residents
D3	U/S not collected as scheduled 3 times or more	
J2	Unemployed more than 5 days	
P6	Violated curfew more than once/week	
D1	More than 1 positive urine	
P1	Restricted to Center 1 or more times	
P3	Police contact	
P10	Arrested	
R3	Parole denied or postponed	

Resident Assessment Scale (Include all residents who lived at CHHDC during this quarter.)

Position	1	2	3	4	5	6	7	8	9	10
No. residents										

Figure 4-4. MIS Quarterly Summary Form

Year

SERD/Congress Heights Human Development Center
406 Condon Terrace, S.E.
Washington, D.C. 20032

MIS ANNUAL SUMMARY FORM

No. residents at beginning of year _____ No. residents at end of year _____

Item		Number residents
D3	U/S not collected as scheduled 3 times or more	
J2	Unemployed more than 5 days	
P6	Violated curfew more than once/week	
D1	More than 1 positive urine	
P1	Restricted to Center 1 or more times	
P3	Police contact	
P10	Arrested	
R3	Parole denied or postponed	

Resident Assessment Scale (Include all residents who lived at SERD/CHHDC during this year.)

Position	1	2	3	4	5	6	7	8	9	10
No. residents										

Figure 4-5. MIS Annual Summary Form

5

A Case Study Evaluation: The SERD/Congress Heights Human Development Center (SERD/CHHDC), 1971-1973

Introduction

Social, Educational Research and Development, Inc. (SERD), is a human development, social science, research, and consulting organization. The firm was created in 1964 to engage in controversial and experimental social and human development programs. Throughout the 1960s, SERD was involved in a variety of projects in the general area of corrections—almost entirely of a research and evaluation variety. In 1971, as a result of a competitive bidding process, the District of Columbia Department of Corrections (DCDC) asked SERD to develop and operate a community correctional center for youthful offenders that:

1. would be located in the Anacostia portion of Washington, D.C.—that part of the District of Columbia with the highest crime rate, but also a part of the City where the Department of Corrections had been unsuccessful in establishing community centers;
2. would explore new approaches, techniques, and experimental efforts, take chances, and develop programs not likely to occur in publicly sponsored community correctional centers.

This report of program results was prepared at the end of the second year of operation of the SERD/Congress Heights Human Development Center (SERD/CHHDC). One of the management approaches that had been introduced at SERD/CHHDC was constant evaluation—self-evaluation and third-party evaluation. Accordingly, SERD has probably amassed more data about the successes and problems of residents, staff, and program operations than are available for any single community correctional center in the United States. These data are vital; the important question in SERD's opinion to be asked of community correctional programs is: Do they make a difference? Or, to turn the coin around, do they rehabilitate the people they serve?

SERD/CHHDC did a good job in fulfilling its original goals, but ways to improve were constantly sought. The Center was located in Anacostia, as requested by the Department of Corrections—a location that provided problems in getting underway. A variety of innovative approaches were developed; most of these approaches were successful. Data are presented in this case study that suggest that SERD/CHHDC may have been the most effective (productively) and efficient (cost-wise) community correctional center for youth in Washington, D.C., between 1971 and 1973. This was the basis for this report.

Highlights of this Case Study

The SERD/Congress Heights Human Development Center was a community center serving youthful offenders 18-24 years of age, under sentence, who were released to the Center by the Youth Services Division of the D.C. Department of Corrections (DCDC). The Center, located in Southeast Washington, D.C., served a maximum of 55 residents on a residential basis and was operated under a contract between Social, Educational Research and Development, Inc. (SERD) and the District of Columbia Department of Corrections. SERD/CHHDC was in operation between June, 1971, and December, 1973.

The case study presents a summary of the effectiveness of operations of SERD/CHHDC between June, 1971, and June, 1973, supported by detailed statistical, comparative, and cost data. To make these data more meaningful, when possible, SERD/CHHDC has been compared to a "sister house," the Community Treatment Center for Youth (CTCY)—a program serving the same population group as SERD/CHHDC but which was operated by the D.C. Department of Corrections.[a] The basic conclusions presented in this report are:

1. *SERD/CHHDC stressed job development.* SERD believed that youth such as these residents had been counseled (psychologically) excessively and essentially nonproductively most of their lives. What they needed most in the short time they spent at SERD/CHHDC was service and support in the job and career areas.
2. *SERD/CHHDC was a client-oriented program.* Stress was placed on viewing failures as staff failures and not as client failures.
3. *SERD/CHHDC was an experimental program.* SERD was willing and eager to try new approaches and from the start did this; some ideas were proven valuable. These approaches are described in this case study.

Some important points noted in this case study are:

1. In February, 1972, *SERD established a Management Information System (MIS)* at SERD/CHHDC. The system was a detailed method for tracking progress and problems of residents. It provided quick and easy data about a given resident during his stay in the program; it enabled comparison of selected problems (jobs, urine surveillance, etc.); and it was a valuable management tool in assessing staff effectiveness.[b]

---

[a]CTCY, operated by the D.C. Department of Corrections, had been in existence for six years as of June, 1973 and is located at 1825 Thirteenth Street, N.W., Washington, D.C. CTCY is licensed to serve 66 residents.

[b]The MIS used is presented here in Chapter 4.

2. *SERD/CHHDC established a modified behavior-modification program*, known as the Credit Advancement Program (CAP).
3. *Because of excessive delays and inaccuracies in reporting the results of urine surveillance tests to denote drug usage, SERD/CHHDC developed a back-up system* in which a private contract with a laboratory provided staff results within 24-hours as opposed to the four- to six-week delay that occurred within the regular program provided by DCDC. This back-up system demonstrated the absolute necessity of quick results of urine samples if surveillance is to be effective.
4. *A detailed Procedures Manual was developed* that described all the steps, procedures, and methods to be followed by each staff person in carrying out their responsibilities and job functions in the program. It provided a high degree of uniformity, accountability, and quick action and/or response on the part of the staff.
5. *A "duty officer" system was developed* and implemented in which staff persons rotated responsibility. One staff person for a week assumed crisis management of the Center at all hours of the day or night.

In terms of program results, the case study reports:

1. During the last few months of FY 1973, the resident population approached the maximum level agreed on with the Department of Corrections—a maximum of 55 residents on a residential basis and 25 on an out-count basis. The maximum possible resident man-days of service in one year's time for SERD/CHHDC was 20,200. In FY 1972, approximately 9,200 man-days of service were provided. In FY 1973, the service doubled—to about 18,200 man-days. However, even in FY 1973, the Center operated considerably below capacity. This is important because if the Center had operated at or near capacity, it would have been able to deliver more efficient and less expensive services.
2. *The success rate of SERD/CHHDC continued to improve; the failure rate continued to decline.*
   —In FY 1972, SERD/CHHDC paroled 26 residents; in FY 1973, more than three times that number, 81, were paroled. (See Tables 5-2 and 5-3.)
   —In FY 1972, SERD/CHHDC paroled about 26 percent of the residents served; CTCY paroled about 28 percent. In FY 1973, SERD/CHHDC paroled about 39 percent and the comparable statistic for CTCY was about 20 percent. (See Tables 5-2 and 5-3.)
   —SERD/CHHDC's parole failure (recidivism) rate for 1972-1973 was about 8 percent compared to about 27 percent for CTCY. (See Table 5-4.)
   —Length-of-time-on-parole data were not available for CTCY, but 84 percent of the 43 people who had been on parole from SERD/CHHDC for more than nine months were still successfully on parole as of June 26, 1973. (See Table 5-5.)
   —In the year ending June, 1973, SERD/CHHDC's cost per man-day was

$21.13; CTCY's cost per man-day was $20.26. However, SERD/CHHDC operated below capacity during most of that period; thus, SERD/CHHDC's costs were higher than they needed to be. During the last half of that year (when SERD/CHHDC was closer to capacity), man-day costs were $19.57 and the comparable cost for CTCY was $20.02. In the event SERD/CHHDC had been able to operate at capacity the entire year, it could have provided average cost per man-day services at about $18 or less. (See Table 5-7.)

The purpose of a community correctional center is to produce the greatest number of successful residents at the least expense. "Successful residents" are offenders who manage to stay free of the criminal justice system. The best indication of this is the extent to which residents who pass through centers successfully can remain on parole. *In FY 1973, costs per successful parolees were: for CTCY, $6,887, and for SERD/CHHDC, $5,278.* SERD estimated that, operating at capacity, SERD/CHHDC could have produced successful parolees at a cost of approximately $5,000 per person or less. This is a most significant conclusion. A national estimate is that it costs $11,000[1] to keep a married man in prison for a year and the recidivism rates for people released directly from prison to parole range from 25-50 percent for youth during the first year.[2] The D.C. Department of Corrections reported costs of $8,465 annually to keep a young man in Youth Center #1 at Lorton.[3] The DCDC figure, of course, does not include lost wages, taxes, etc., for this incarcerated person.

SERD/CHHDC Population Movement

An Overview

Data in this section present the population characteristics and patterns of SERD/CHHDC residents during Fiscal Years 1972 and 1973. Generally, FY 1973 data are a better measure of performance because the population was nearer capacity toward the latter part of that year.[c] Also, in most programs of this type, the first year of operation is considered a start-up period and analyses of first year operations usually show higher costs and less stability.

The D.C. Department of Corrections operated or provided funding for nine adult community centers and two youth centers in addition to SERD/CHHDC.[d] One of the most enduring problems in social service programs is the relative impact of programs coordinated by public and private agencies. DCDC operated

---

[c]FY 1973 data, for the year ending June 30, 1973, represent actual data up to June 15, 1973. Time periods beyond that date represent estimates.

[d]In addition, Shaw Residence #3, funded by DCDC, opened in August, 1970, and was operated by the Bureau of Rehabilitation as a youth facility from September, 1971, to April, 1972.

a community center, CTCY, serving almost the same type of population as SERD/CHHDC. Therefore, when data are available, SERD/CHHDC has been compared its "sister house"—the Community Treatment Center for Youth (CTCY). CTCY opened in June, 1967; it was a fully operational program completing its sixth year of operation in June, 1973. Capacity at CTCY was 66[e] residents on an in-count basis.

Youth Progress House (previously the Youth Crime Control Project) was an experimental program that allowed offenders to serve their entire sentence in the community. Capacity for in-count residents at Youth Progress House (YPH) was 30. Where possible throughout this report and when information was available, SERD/CHHDC's performance has been compared with that of both CTCY and YPH. The YPH program, however, was somewhat different from those of both SERD and CTCY.[4]

It should be emphasized that the sixth year of operation of CTCY is being compared to the second year of operation for SERD/CHHDC.[f] These comparisons are some of the most significant aspects of this study. Insofar as SERD could ascertain, this is the first occasion in which a publicly operated program has been compared with a private program.

Resident Man-days of Service

In FY 1972, because of an unsettled zoning issue, the District of Columbia government imposed a maximum limit on SERD/CHHDC of 25 residents on an in-count basis. The issue was resolved in June, 1972, and during FY 1973, SERD/CHHDC operated with an occupancy permit and license for a maximum of 55 residents.

Table 5-1 provides general population movement data for SERD/CHHDC and CTCY. In the first year of operation (FY 1972), SERD/CHHDC admitted a total of 101 residents as compared to 210 new admissions in FY 1973, for an average monthly admission record of 8.5 in 1972 versus 17.5 in 1973. Table 5-1 indicates a continuing overall increase in residents qualifying for out-count under the terms of the Credit Advancement Program (CAP) which was initiated on August 1, 1972; 32 percent of total man-days at SERD/CHHDC during FY 1973 were spent in out-count status as opposed to 21.1 percent during FY 1972. During FY 1973, CTCY provided a total of 21,413 resident man-days of service, of which 14,028, or 65.5 percent were in-count man-days, and 7,385, or 34.5 percent, were out-count man-days.[g]

The average monthly population for SERD/CHHDC during FY 1973 was 48.

---

[e]The FY 1972 rooming house license for CTCY authorized 66 residents. No information regarding license capacity was available for FY 1973.

[f]See Appendix A for detailed methods and techniques used in this case study.

[g]CTCY population data were not available for FY 1972.

Table 5-1
SERD/CHHDC and CTCY Population Data by Resident Man-days for Quarter-years, FY 1972 and 1973[a]

Quarter	SERD/CHHDC Total Resident man-days	Total in-count man-days Number	Percent of total	Total out-count man-days Number	Percent of total	CTCY Total resident man-days	Total in-count man-days Number	Percent of total	Total out-count man-days Number	Percent of total
July-September, 1971	1,745	1,697	97.2	48	2.8					
October-December, 1971	1,942	1,721	88.6	221	11.4					
January-March, 1972	2,736	2,006	73.3	730	26.7					
April-June, 1972	2,730	1,802	66.0	928	34.0					
Annual totals FY 1972	9,153	7,226	78.9	1,927	21.1					
July-September, 1972	3,170	2,138	67.4	1,032	32.6	5,195	3,325	64.0	1,870	36.0
October-December, 1972	4,342	2,609	60.1	1,733	39.9	5,384	3,319	61.6	2,065	38.4
January-March, 1973	4,953	3,282	66.3	1,671	33.7	4,613	3,055	66.2	1,558	33.8
April-June, 1973[a]	5,768	4,378	75.9	1,390	24.1	6,221	4,329	69.6	1,892	30.4
Annual Totals FY 1973	18,233	12,407	68.0	5,826	32.0	21,413	14,028	65.5	7,385	34.5

[a]See Appendix A for methodological statement, assumptions, bases for, and validity of these data.

For the same period, CTCY averaged 56 residents each month. During January through June, 1973 (the last half of the year), SERD/CHHDC was operating at nearer capacity than previously with a monthly average population of 55 out of a maximum of 80.[h]

Intake and Movement of Residents

Table 5-2 presents population data for FY 1972 for the three programs.

Tables 5-2 and 5-3 present significant population movement comparisons between SERD/CHHDC and CTCY for 1972-1973.

—Parole rates: SERD/CHHDC's number of paroles increased by three times from 1972 to 1973, though population only doubled. Parolees as a percentage of persons served increased for SERD/CHHDC from 25.7 percent in 1972 to 38.6 percent in 1973. For CTCY the rate decreased from 28.3 percent in 1972 to 27.3 percent in 1973.
—Failure rates for both centers declined from 1972 to 1973. For SERD/CHHDC, the decline was from 41.6 percent to 30.5 percent and for CTCY, the comparable data were 40.0 percent and 36.5 percent.

The important point to note in Tables 5-2 and 5-3 is that CTCY, as an established facility with over five years of experience, had about the same

Table 5-2
Population Movement: DCDC Youth Services Community Correctional Centers—FY 1972[a]

	SERD/CHHDC		YPH		CTCY	
Item	Number	Percent	Number	Percent	Number	Percent
Paroles	26	25.7	17	19.3	97	28.3
In-program failures	42	41.6	43	48.9	136	40.0
Other actions	2	2.0	0	0	3	0.8
In program at June 30, 1972	31	30.7	28	31.8	60	17.5
Unaccounted for	0	0	0	0	46	13.4
Total residents	101	100.0	88	100.0	342	100.0

[a]See Appendix A for methodological statement, assumptions, bases for, and validity of these data.

---

[h]For SERD/CHHDC, capacity is 29,200 man-days of service in a year. Thus in FY 1973, SERD/CHHDC operated at 37.5 percent below capacity (see Table 5-1).

Table 5-3
Population Movement: SERD/CHHDC and CTCY—FY 1973[a]

Item	July 1, 1972-June 30, 1973					January 1-June 30, 1973				
	SERD/CHHDC		CTCY			SERD/CHHDC		CTCY	
	Number	Percent	Number	Percent		Number	Percent	Number	Percent
Paroles	81	38.6	86	27.3		45	31.0	38	19.8
In-program failures	64	30.5	115	36.5		39	26.9	59	30.7
Other actions	6	2.8	0	0		2	1.4	0	0
In program at June 30, 1973	59	28.1	70	22.2		59	40.7	70	36.5
Unaccounted for	0	0	44	14.0		0	0	25	13.0
Total	210	100.0	315	100.0		145	100.0	192	100.0

[a]See Appendix A for methodological statement, assumptions, bases for, and validity of these data.

program results as did SERD/CHHDC in its first year of operation. In its second year of operation, SERD/CHHDC exceeded CTCY in its proportion of paroles and produced a lower failure rate, and by the time SERD/CHHDC population came nearer capacity (during the last six months of 1973), SERD/CHHDC's results far exceeded the CTCY record in these two crucial areas.

An issue not discussed in any detail in this report, but one that is serious, is the problem of residents who were "multiple in-program failures." SERD/CHHDC had, since opening the program, 106 failures. This represented 86 individuals; 47 of the 86 individuals failed more than once. What occurred with these failures was a cyclical process—youth institution to community center to youth institution to community center, etc. Two things were needed. First, centers should have had the option of returning problem residents to the youth centers or the jail for short periods of adjustment time, and second, separate programs should have been developed for multiple failures.

Program Successes

The most significant data to evaluate the effectiveness of community correctional centers are the rates of success. SERD/CHHDC had been in operation 24 months (on June 30, 1973). The first resident went on parole in October, 1971. Since that date, SERD/CHHDC paroled 107 residents—53.6 percent of the total population in 1973. As noted in Table 5-3 in 1973, SERD/CHHDC was paroling 38.6 percent of its population and CTCY was paroling 27.3 percent. More important is parolee recidivism. The data for both CTCY and SERD/CHHDC for 1972 and 1973 are presented in Table 5-4. The data in Table 5-4 indicate SERD/CHHDC's parole failure or recidivism rate averaged 8.4 percent; for CTCY, it averaged 27.3 percent.

Another important measure of program success is the length of time a person

Table 5-4
Parole and Recidivism Data: SERD/CHHDC and CTCY[a]

| | SERD/CHHDC | | | CTCY | | | |
| | | Recidivists | | | Recidivists | | |
Period	Paroles	Number	Percent	Paroles	Number	Percent	Status unknown
FY 1972	26	1	3.8	97	29	31.9	6
FY 1973	81	8	9.9	86	18	22.2	5
Total	107	9	8.4	183	47	27.3	11

[a]See Appendix A for methodological statement, assumptions, bases for, and validity of these data.

Table 5-5
Time on Parole for SERD/CHHDC Parolees as of June 26, 1973 [a]

Length of time to date of recidivism as of June 26, 1973	Still on parole Number	Still on parole Percent	Recidivists Number	Recidivists Percent	Total Number	Total Percent
18 months or longer	6	100.0	0	0	6	100
Over 12, but less than 18 months	17	85.0	3	15.0	20	100
Over 9, but less than 12 months	13	76.5	4	23.5	17	100
Over 6, but less than 9 months	18	9.5	1	5.3	19	100
6 months or less	44	97.8	1	2.2	45	100
Total	98	91.6	9	8.4	107	100

[a]See Appendix B for methodological statement, assumptions, bases for, and validity of these data.

remains on parole upon release from a community center. Data were available for all SERD/CHHDC former residents; such data were not available from CTCY.

Comparable data from other programs are difficult to come by. The Uniform Parole Reports produced these national data: in 1967, 49 percent of youth with drug histories were successful parolees after one year; in 1973, the comparable statistic was 56 percent.[5]

SERD/CHHDC Resident Employment and Earnings

At SERD/CHHDC the employment rate (including enrollment in full-time training or educational programs) during the first year of operation was 44.2 percent of the maximum number of employable days. Due to increased emphasis by staff on this vital aspect of the SERD/CHHDC program, the employment rate jumped to 62.8 percent during the first 11 months of the second year. SERD believed that continued improvement—both in the number and percent of days of employment by residents—and in the residents' earning potential was possible and realistic; career development, therefore, was to be a key program objective as the program moved into its third year of operation.

Gross earnings reported by SERD/CHHDC residents during the first year of operation totaled $33,586.04, compared to $72,226.62 in the first 11 months of the second year.[i] The improvement in this sector can be better appreciated by comparing average monthly earnings for the two periods:

$2,798.84 per month, FY 1972
$6,566.06 per month, FY 1973

In Fiscal Year 1972, the average hourly wage rate for employed residents was $2.38 per hour.[j] In FY 1973, the average hourly rate had increased to $2.60 per hour—an increase of 9 percent.[k] This increase may be partially attributable to increases in minimum wage rates, but that is unlikely because jobs generally held by residents were low-level, unskilled jobs that oftentimes paid wages below the minimum. While much improvement in this area can be attributed to the increase in occupancy level and the substantial improvement effected in the employment rate, some of the improvement must also be credited to the intensified job counseling and improvements in wage-recording methods that occurred at SERD/CHHDC during FY 1973.

Employed residents paid a nominal subsistence to the program that was returned to DCDC to offset program costs. During 1972-1973, approximately $1,000 was collected. Increased efforts in record-keeping and collections in this area in 1973 indicated these collections might have reached $200 to $300 per month during FY 1974.

Even more important was the fact that increasing wage rates for residents and placing them in higher level jobs with a career ladder would result in increases in future taxes collected by the D.C. and federal governments. For example, during FY 1973 residents contributed $3,327.54 to Social Security and paid $8,298.30 in federal and state taxes.[l] During the entire operation of the Center, residents contributed $4,660.05 in Social Security and $10,865.32 in federal and state taxes. If Social Security contributions and taxes paid during the period January through May, 1973 (when population was nearer capacity), are projected, it would be safe to assume that the figures for FY 1974 would approach $350 per month for Social Security and $850 per month paid by employed residents in federal and state taxes. If, from the total operating costs of the SERD/CHHDC program, annual deductions are made of these amounts—federal and state taxes paid by employed residents and subsistence collections of $10,200 and $2,800, respectively—this reduces the operating costs of the program by at least $13,000.

---

[i]Note that approximately 20 percent of SERD/CHHDC residents were considered "employed" because they were enrolled in education and/or training programs. However, some were not receiving wages or paying taxes.

[j]Hourly wage-rate data were not available for January through June, 1972.

[k]Data for June, 1973, were not available and are not included.

[l]June, 1973, figures were not included.

Social Security contributions of employed residents provide an additional reduction of $4,200.

Urine Surveillance

The overwhelming majority of residents passing through SERD/CHHDC had been "hard drug" or heroin users. To deal with this problem generally, the D.C. Department of Corrections conducted a urine surveillance program for all community correctional centers. The procedures worked somewhat as follows. Staff collected urine samples on a periodic basis (at SERD/CHHDC, samples were collected from all residents three times each week). The urine samples were then collected by a laboratory under contract with the Department of Corrections. The laboratory processed the samples and reported the results to the Department, which, in turn, reported the results to the centers. SERD/CHHDC was plagued with two serious problems regarding the urine surveillance program. The problems and SERD's solutions were as follows.

1. *The collection of samples and program monitoring:* The SERD/CHHDC Procedures Manual described in detail urine surveillance program procedures that all staff were required to follow. The essential elements were that all residents were required to produce urine samples at selected times. Samples were taken in a bathroom set aside specifically for that purpose. Only one resident was permitted in the bathroom at a time, and the collection of the sample was observed directly by the House Supervisor on duty. Next, collected samples were stored in a locked refrigerator. Following the collection of the samples, the resident and the House Supervisor each initialed the urine sample list. These highly specific and detailed procedures and the recording forms that accompanied them, in SERD's judgment, immeasurably increased the accuracy of the collection and recording system. In fact, staff were confident that recording and collection errors had, for all practical purposes, been eliminated from the program due to these procedures.

2. By far the most serious problem was the time lag from the collection of a sample to the reporting date. In 1972 and early 1973, the time lag had increased from four to six weeks. In mid-1973, the lag was reduced to three to four weeks. A successful urine surveillance program could occur only when there was absolute assurance of the validity of the data collected and when the results were reported back immediately. Accordingly, in late 1972, SERD contracted with a private laboratory to provide urinalysis results on a same-day basis. The agreement was that the laboratory would pick up samples in the morning and telephone the results the same day. This proved to be an immensely valuable tool in dealing with drug abuse on a selective basis.

Even though there was incomplete reporting of results in FY 1972, 63 of 390 residents tested that year (or 16.1 percent) had two or more unauthorized positive urines in a given month.[m] Other improvements apparent from statistics in every facet of the SERD/CHHDC operation cannot compare with the great advances made in the narcotics surveillance area. Only 27 of 529 men tested during the first 10 months of FY 1973 had two or more unauthorized positive urines—or 5.1 percent *versus* 16.1 percent for the previous year. Staff attributed this very substantial improvement to three factors:

1. the "spot checking" of suspected drug users through the separate contract between SERD and a local laboratory to supplement the Department's standard urine surveillance program;
2. the implementation of the Credit Advancement Program; and
3. the intensive counseling and close personal supervision given to suspected drug users by the treatment staff.

Comparative Cost Data: SERD/CHHDC and CTCY

An Overview

One of the most controversial issues in social service fields is the relative efficiency (cost) and effectiveness (success) of private versus public programs. SERD assembled cost data that compares SERD/CHHDC and CTCY in terms of these two variables. The conclusions and supporting data are included in this section and, briefly summarized, are:

— SERD/CHHDC in 1973 was producing successful parolees at a cost of $5,278; CTCY's cost was $6,887.
— SERD/CHHDC services in 1973 cost $21.13 per man-day; CTCY's costs were $20.26. If SERD/CHHDC had operated at capacity in 1973, the estimated man-day cost would have been about $18.
— The total dollar cost for SERD/CHHDC in 1973 was approximately $385,320; for CTCY, it was approximately $433,850.

These results are reported in the two sections that follow; Appendix A contains the basis for these results and data collection methodology.

Comparison of Costs per Successful Parolee

The costs per successful parolee for SERD/CHHDC and CTCY in FY 1973 are compared in Table 5-6. This table also shows the number and percentages of

---
[m]Authorized "positives" included medical prescriptions if the resident was under a doctor's care and methadone if the resident was participating in a methadone maintenance program; all other "positive" results were unauthorized.

Table 5-6
Comparison of SERD/CHHDC and CTCY Costs per Successful Parolee—FY 1973[a]

Item	SERD/CHHDC	CTCY
Number of paroles	81	86
Number of paroles revoked	8	18
Percent of paroles revoked	9.9%	22.2%
Number of successful paroles	73	63
Percent of successful paroles	90.1%	77.8%
Total cost for FY 1973	$385,316	$433,854
Cost per successful parolee	$5,278	$6,887

[a]See Appendix A for methodological statement, assumptions, bases for, and validity of these data.

successful and unsuccessful parolees for each center in FY 1973. SERD had 81 parolees in FY 1973, of which 73 or 90.1 percent were successful as of June, 1973. The D.C. Parole Board reported that CTCY paroled 86 in FY 1973, but the status of only 81 parolees could be determined on the basis of available information. Of these 81 parolees, 63 or 77.8 percent were successful, and 18 had failed by June, 1973. The failure rate of CTCY parolees (22.2 percent) was more than double the rate for SERD/CHHDC parolees (9.9 percent).

On the basis of known successful paroles during FY 1973 and total costs incurred during this period, the cost per successful parolee was $5,278 for SERD/CHHDC and $6,887 for CTCY—30 percent higher in the CTCY program than for the SERD/CHHDC program.

Comparison of Costs per Man-day

A comparison of SERD/CHHDC and CTCY costs per man-day for treatment in FY 1973 is shown in Table 5-7. For FY 1973, costs per man-day, based on in-count residents only, was $31.06 for SERD/CHHDC and $30.93 for CTCY. However, for the last half of the fiscal year, SERD/CHHDC costs per man-day, based on in-count, dropped to $27.39 while CTCY's costs declined to $29.38. The last half of the fiscal year is considered to be most relevant for a comparison of costs because SERD/CHHDC operated substantially below capacity during the first half of the year and population was nearer capacity between January and June, 1973, still about 37.5 percent below capacity. At full capacity, SERD/CHHDC's cost per man-day could be expected to drop by about 10 to 20 percent below the level experienced in the last half of FY 1973 or by about $2 to $5 per man-day.

Table 5-7
Comparison of SERD/CHHDC and CTCY Costs per Man-day—FY 1973[a]

Program and period	Number of man-days			Total cost for period	Cost per man-day	
	In-count	Out-count	Total		In-count	Total
SERD/CHHDC						
July 1, 1972-June 30, 1973	12,407	5,826	18,233	$385,316	$31.06	$21.13
January 1, 1973-June 30, 1973	7,660	3,061	10,721	$209,815	$27.39	$19.57
CTCY						
July 1, 1972-June 30, 1973	14,028	7,385	21,413	$433,854	$30.93	$20.26
January 1, 1973-June 30, 1973	7,385	3,450	10,835	$216,927	$29.38	$20.02

[a]See Appendix A for methodological statement, assumptions, bases for, and validity of these data.

Evaluation

CAP and MIS afforded excellent opportunities for assessment and evaluation of the SERD/CHHDC program. Also, during FY 1973, several evaluation studies were undertaken.

The MIS and the data generated by it permitted SERD to conduct a number of small, problem-specific studies. First, a weekly analysis of MIS data enabled identification of those residents who were having specific problems as well as those who were having problems in more than one area and who, therefore, needed special attention. By reversing the data, it was possible to identify those residents whose behavior in the three critical areas—urine surveillance, employment, and curfew violation—suggested the need for immediate staff attention. This weekly report was, of course, in addition to daily reviews of MIS data conducted by SERD/CHHDC management staff.

SERD completed many MIS studies. For instance, in one study ten residents who were "top" performers were compared with ten residents who performed at the other end of the scale. It was learned that successful residents spent significantly less time at the Center than did failures; that they attained employment almost immediately upon arrival; that they failed to give urine samples only 25 percent as frequently as failures; that failures had ten times as many unauthorized positive, or "dirty" urine samples as did successes; that it was rarely necessary to restrict successful residents to the Center (i.e., those who failed were restricted 30 times more often than were successes); that failures were guilty of curfew violations 15 times more frequently than were successes; and that failures failed to call in almost twice as frequently as did successes. Findings from these studies permitted SERD to make predictions on the basis of early performance at the Center and to give special attention to those whose behavior during the early part of their stay suggested this need. Another study conducted on the basis of MIS data was a comparative study of two caseloads. This study followed the termination of employment of one counselor. The termination action was found to be very wise because in retrospect, suspicions were confirmed—that a successful counselor had four times as many program successes as the counselor who was terminated and only one-third the failures (arrests, escapes, and remands).

A list of the evaluative studies undertaken and the date each study was completed follows.

1. August 16, 1972: SERD/CHHDC Management Review conducted August 14, 1972
2. September 11, 1972: A Comparative Study of Two Counseling Caseloads from March 13-June 15, 1972
3. September 21, 1972: A Review of Management Information Data Collected on 20 Program Failures, February 1-July 13, 1972

4. September 28, 1972: Review of the Credit Advancement Program
5. November 17, 1972: Resident Population on Weekends
6. December 20, 1972: A Review of Management Information Data Collected on 26 Residents Who Achieved Parole During the Period February 1-July 31, 1972
7. January 8, 1973: A Look at Two Extremes in Resident Behavior Patterns
8. January 18, 1973: Reports, Resident Funds, Urine Surveillance Rules and Regulations of Out-count Residents
9. February 8, 1973: Resident Information Report (FY 1972) Prepared for Youth Services Division
10. February 12, 1973: Supplemental Resident Information Report (FY 1972) Prepared for Youth Services Division
11. February 20, 1973: Review of Resident Loan Fund at SERD/CHHDC, June 23, 1971-January 31, 1973
12. March 1, 1973: SERD/CHHDC Monthly Billing Record Verification, February, 1973
13. March 26, 1973: Intensive Review of MIS Monthly and Quarterly Reports
14. March 29, 1973: Intensive Analysis of MIS Weekly Report, March 12-18, 1973
15. April 3, 1973: Intensive Analysis of MIS Weekly Report, March 19-25, 1973
16. April 10, 1973: Intensive Analysis of MIS Weekly Report, March 26-April 1, 1973
17. April 17, 1973: Audit of SERD/CHHDC Petty Cash Fund, March 1-April 2, 1973
18. April 23, 1973: Intensive Analysis of MIS Weekly Report, April 2-8, 1973
19. April 24, 1973: Intensive Analysis of MIS Weekly Report, April 9-15, 1973
20. April 25, 1973: Report of Meeting with Cooks and Recommendations for Improvement of Food Program Operations
21. April 26, 1973: Combined CAP/MIS Record Recommendations
22. April 27, 1973: Weekly Token Reports Review, March 30-April 27, 1973
23. May 1, 1973: "Dirty" Urines, January-March, 1973
24. May 8, 1973: A Statistical Overview of the SERD/Congress Heights Human Development Center, July 1, 1971-March 31, 1973
25. May 10, 1973: Audit of CHHDC Petty Cash and Transportation Tokens, April 3-30, 1973
26. May 17, 1973: Subsistence Collections since April 17, 1973, and Recommendations for Procedures

An evaluation of the Credit Advancement Program was conducted in FY 1973 by a behavior-oriented research organization. This resulted in further refinement of the program, restructuring of staff and resident bonus systems, and additional planning for an advanced staff training program for the Program Division staff. The evaluation also recommended combining MIS and CAP reporting forms to avoid duplication and conflicts in reporting data. By spring, 1973, the revisions were in the process of being completed, staff had reviewed copies of the revised form, and a manual describing entries was being prepared.

Because drug abuse was such a pervasive factor in the history of most residents, it received a great deal of attention at both the policy and program levels at SERD/CHHDC. To aid in assessing the effectiveness of this aspect of the program, in fall, 1973, SERD engaged the services of a drug treatment expert. In his report he stated:

The . . . SERD halfway house design is very impressive. It attempts to merge all known program strategies for . . . addiction into (one) . . . model using various treatment modalities. The average stay is measured in weeks before exit from the . . . program, so it deserves the closest study from the point of view of social outcome measurements; i.e., arrest rates, employment patterns, etc., as well as from a cost-benefit analysis. It is impressive . . . that while the SERD . . . house has had the usual problems seen in other urban cities, the willingness of the parent organization as well as the . . . staff to examine their own behavior, allow their behavior to be examined by an outsider, and the . . . feeling that competency can only be achieved by an intensive review of the program failures hold well in the quest for competency.

A chronic disabling problem to the program has been that very few clients have had much of a work record and the level of marketable labor skills, on the average, is minimal. An additional problem arises due to the fact that a successful client is away from the house for many hours during the day. The nature of the program means that the analysis of the client's behavior is not a 24-hour-a-day residential model and, therefore, more indirect measurements have to be used. The Management Information System (MIS) has been a remarkable development in this program. This data system measures, on a daily basis, many aspects of behavior which are put into a weekly summary. In this writer's opinion, this is one of the best management systems that he has seen. The next step is to consider how the data can be incorporated into the ongoing operational decision-making process of the halfway house.

To keep the data system alive and useful, it must be used. One design is to have the day start off at the house with a meeting between the Director, Chief of Programs, Chief of Operations, and some process devised to get feedback from the evening and night staff. The evening staff interacts and sees the residents in a very immediate sense due to the nature of the program. Such a daily meeting could focus on immediate and urgent problems that have arisen in the previous 24 hours in the house.

The growth of the halfway house is urban 'normal' in other respects; the quest for competency has resulted in the usual . . . staff turnover. Presently, there is a very strong management group at the house with considerable experience, shrewdness, and competency. A very serious and potentially destructive problem has arisen over the urine surveillance program; the time lag between urine collection and reporting is measured in weeks. This would mean that a client can be well along in the process of becoming strung out again before this can be detected by the urine screening test. For urine surveillance to have relevance in the treatment center, the reports have to be available within a day or two after the urine has been taken. This allows a very prompt and early confrontation with the client about his drug problem and thus consideration of several alternatives in order to prevent the inevitable arrest or return to the street life and criminality seen with addiction.

A very interesting program strategy has arisen in the halfway house which is called the Credit Advancement Program (CAP). This program allows the client to advance through certain phases if he accumulates points. One immediate effect of this program, now that advancement is automatic, is that the counseling staff has noticed a marked reduction in the hassles around privileges, etc. This reduction is causing a change in the interaction between the counselor and client, and the counseling contacts are now becoming much more concerned with the underlying and longer term problems of the client.

A site visit evaluation was also conducted by a sociologist. Excerpts from his report follow.

Jobs are the major task focus of ... counselors. It is not clear to me to what extent the criteria used for hiring counselors has reflected this focus. How much thought has been given to the best way to find jobs; who is most likely to be able to do this, with what kinds of assistance? What kinds of rewards are given to counselors who find the 'approved' kinds of jobs, or who develop improved techniques for finding jobs? Has any thought been given to the development of a network of "spotters" who are suitably rewarded for providing information leading to the identification of a bona fide job opening?

... The counselor position is (soon) to be restructured (just how, or in what ways is not specified), and the job title is to be changed. Is the implication that this will be enough to change the self-definition of the hitherto counselors, and to change their behavior?

... "Program and staff will be measured in terms of the time it will take to place residents as well as the quality of the jobs residents receive." This is an honorable statement, but one that can lead to trouble. Some residents will be a lot easier to place than others; some residents will be a lot more willing to stay with a job than others. Staff members can quickly become demoralized (more important, find ways of evading the onus) if they are held responsible for conditions over which they have little control. More dangerous, perhaps, there will be little incentive to stick with the tough cases. It may be possible to develop some kind of weighting scale so that staff member 'scores' on job placement will include a factor for difficulty—as does the scoring system in diving competition.

... How are "backsliders" to be treated? To what extent are those who ... move back into an earlier phase, treated differently? ... I have the feeling, based on admittedly little knowledge, that heavy reliance is placed on the point system to carry this burden.

... There has been a problem of turnover.... to the extent that the environment is consciously structured, as well. That is to say, what model for administration would appear to be most related to the goals and principles of the organization? At one extreme the total therapeutic community has been rejected. One would presume that the prison model, with its extreme hierarchy likewise is ... inappropriate. But to what extent has consideration been given to the fit between the structure of administration and the goals of the organization?

... The counselors are on the front line, supported by the house supervisors. . . . It is simply not clear to me how much guidance, and with what effectiveness, passes up and down this line. . . . If the model of administration that is held is: "I know best; you follow orders," or if the situation is defined as too filled with crises to permit consultation, then this may be appropriate. On the other hand, if there is a desire to build team work and a sense of mutual support, then opportunities for formal staff interaction must be provided. . . .

Staff meetings can serve to better integrate the program and operations functions. They . . . provide a legitimate avenue for the involvement in program concerns of some persons in operations who feel the need for a more direct participation in the goals of the organization.

It may be that MIS data have only recently become reliable, and therefore elaborate statistical analysis is premature. However, it would seem to me that a great deal could be gained if a cohort presentation were prepared in addition to the weekly presentation. That is, records could be prepared beginning with week #1 for each resident. In a short time, there would be enough data, that is, enough cases, for the development of graphs representing the typical progress for successes, failures, and those holding the middle ground. A comparison of these graphs might well highlight crucial turning points in the careers of residents. Such evidence could reinforce, or replace, the current rule of thumb that if a resident does not get a job in three weeks, he is likely to end up a failure.

As I see it, the most important missing information concerning the operation of the program has to do with the interaction between the residents and the staff, and the extent to which that process has something to do with the outcomes measured in various ways. . . .

Implications of this Case Study

This study has several implications: First, it should be very clear that SERD/CHHDC was a viable and effective program. The data presented here indicate very strongly that the SERD program was providing high-quality services at a relatively low cost.

Second, this project had in two years, produced a variety of new ideas, techniques, and approaches, not the least of which was a data system that probably was the most efficient and capable to be found in any community correctional center in the United States. This and other approaches included:

—SERD/CHHDC had designed, tested, and developed a Management Information System (MIS) that enabled quick and efficient tracking of residents throughout the program and evaluation of staff services to residents.
—A cohort system of evaluation had been developed that compared the progress of groups of residents who entered the program in six-month time periods.
—A modified behavior-modification program (CAP) had been developed and was in use. This program proved to be unusually effective and efficient in motivating residents to move through the program quickly.
—A Policy and Procedures Manual had been written that covered in great detail,

all the procedures, requirements, needs, and emergency processes for staff in the SERD/CHHDC program.[n]
- The "duty officer" concept had been developed and successfully implemented. This procedure assigned a key staff person on a weekly basis to provide policy and crisis management to the Center during evenings, weekends, and at other times when key staff were unavailable.
- A number of procedures and processes had been developed, including a revised Parole Progress Report Form that enabled careful collection and reporting of data, more efficient assessment of residents, and a smoother review process for the Parole Board.
- During the early stages of this program, SERD led the effort to develop, in the District of Columbia, a realistic zoning and licensing regulation and procedure for community correctional centers. Such a regulation and procedures now exist.

Third, a major implication of this study is that there should be clearer, more consistent, and more long-term relations between and among various community correctional centers in the District. For example, the Department of Corrections should demand a higher degree of excellence from privately funded operations. Also, there should be joint efforts between community centers involving, for example, such things as staffing exchanges, joint training programs, long and short-term evaluation programs, sharing of information, and common operating procedures. SERD developed an evaluation system that produced more than 26 internal evaluation studies that examined various aspects of the SERD/CHHDC program.

Finally, there needs to be developed in the District of Columbia, a number of new approaches and experimental efforts involving community correctional centers. The Department of Corrections should require that private contractors take the initiative in developing these procedures.

- There is not much evidence that major employers in the District are willing to hire residents of community centers; community centers should take the initiative to persuade them to do so.
- There needs to be careful evaluation of the effectiveness of community centers, especially in terms of private versus public programs, various treatment approaches, etc.
- There should be new kinds of services in community correctional centers. The foster home concept seems like a sensible idea and should be explored, developed, and refined.
- There should be more flexible policies in dealing with behavior problems of

---
[n]This manual had been in use in other centers in the District of Columbia as a model for developing their own manuals.

residents; for instance, it should be possible for community centers to send a resident who is not adjusting, to the jail for a period of three days to several weeks. This would eliminate the process of sending all failures (minor or major) back to the youth institution where little or nothing will happen in terms of rehabilitation. When this resident returns to the community center unchanged a few weeks later, he sometimes is returned again to the Youth Center, and the cycle goes on and on. Perhaps there should be a separate facility that serves these difficult cases or a separate selection process for them.
—Coed facilities: When tried elsewhere, coed programs have been successful. There were no facilities (as of June, 1973) in the District for female Youth Act cases.
—The operation of some private programs should be performance-based.

Proposed Plans for SERD/CHHDC for FY 1973-1974

Generally, the SERD/CHHDC program had been stabilized during FY 1973. However, there were new areas on which the program hoped to focus during FY 1974.º The organizational structure is simple, functional, and adaptable but should be assessed in terms of the sociologist's conclusions noted in the Evaluation Section. Also, in terms of MIS and CAP, the organizational structure had become increasingly important. The Operations Division, for example, was expected to generate reports assessing the effectiveness of the Program Services Division. In addition, CAP required extensive reporting efforts on the part of both Divisions. The Program Services Division carried out CAP and recorded information and the Operations Division transmitted, generated, and analyzed data about the program and residents. The following plans had emerged for FY 1974.

1. *Increasing staff accountability and responsibility:* A Management-by-Objectives (MBO) program would be implemented. This is essentially an effort whereby staff goals and responsibilities are specified in measurable terms and linked to a timetable. Goals would be identified for all staff, and the MIS and other techniques would be used to measure the extent to which objectives were achieved. This MBO program would interface with PROMPT, a reporting system developed by the Department of Corrections for application to all programs within the Department in addition to those under contract. Again, the primary focus would be on employment with particular attention to those program components directly and indirectly related to employment of residents.

2. *Staff and resident incentives:* In the fall of 1972, a staff and resident incentive program was worked out in conjunction with both residents and staff

---

ºA cutback in funding resulted in the closing of the Center in December, 1973, so that all the plans presented here were not implemented.

that called for payments of $500 to the staff and $500 to the residents for any month during which there were no escapes, rearrests, and remands. A series of meetings of both groups was held to determine how they wished to handle the program and both groups decided on a lottery system, i.e., a limited number of names would be "drawn from a hat" and those whose names were drawn would divide the $500 allocated each group. Unfortunately, there were no 30-day periods during which the groups qualified for the reward. Both staff and residents had asked SERD staff for suggestions regarding an incentive program that would be more responsive to the performance of both groups. Several possible alternative plans were being prepared for testing in FY 1974.

3. *Staff training:* During FY 1974, staff training was to be intensified in view of the modified program plan for the year. The new Policy and Procedures Manual was, of course, a basic document for all staff and a minimum of six sessions were planned to review it. Immediately following completion of that training, a weekend seminar would be held on management-by-objectives at which time program and individual objectives would be reviewed and staff would be trained in utilization of that management approach. Revision of the MIS basic reporting form to include CAP would also require training, some of which had already been conducted or was underway. In addition, counseling staff were to be trained in both group and individual career development techniques. Materials that had been and would be developed for this training would also be utilized in orientation and training of new staff who may be employed during FY 1974.

4. *Plan for resident employment program:* Plans were underway to convene a panel of job-development and placement experts whose recommendations would be utilized to strengthen this portion of the program. The panel would include a member from the Department of Corrections, the Employment Service, the Department of Labor, and representatives from private industry and other relevant government agencies. Issues to be addressed included:

a. staff training and career development,
b. development of work opportunities with private employers,
c. strategies for relating to major employers,
d. strategies for relating to smaller concerns with high potential for resident employment, and
e. employer and employee incentives.

5. *Parole supervision:* SERD had proposed to DCDC that SERD/CHHDC assume responsibility for supervision of men paroled from the SERD/CHHDC program. During FY 1973, there were several indications (and these were supported by comments from parole officers) that residents tended to "let down" on their employment aspirations upon parole. While on in-count or out-count status, the SERD/CHHDC Credit Advancement Program required that residents maintain employment or be "demoted" to an earlier, less privileged

phase. SERD proposed to continue the same general requirement for parolees except that they would be afforded additional time to obtain employment in the event they became unemployed. For example, in FY 1973, men on out-count who were dismissed from employment on the basis of their performance or lack of performance, were required to return to in-count immediately, and after steady employment had been demonstrated again, they could be returned to out-count. In the event employment was lost through no fault of the resident (e.g., funding cutback, weather, or project completion), the out-count resident was permitted five days in which to obtain another job. Failure to do so resulted in his return to in-count status. For parolees, the same general philosophy would be followed and the details, of course, would be subject to approval of both the Department of Corrections and the Parole Board. All reports required about the parolee by either Department of Corrections staff or the Parole Board would be provided. Continuity within the SERD/CHHDC program would enable staff to respond more quickly to crises arising with parolees than was possible with no responsibility for residents following parole. If SERD/CHHDC assumed parole responsibility for residents as they were paroled, it was estimated that approximately eight to ten parolees per month would be included in the program.

6. *Volunteer program:* Volunteers today constitute a significant work force in the criminal justice system, as individuals and in groups. Estimates are that volunteers outnumber paid workers in the system four to one.[6] About 70 percent of criminal justice agencies have some sort of volunteer program. But many of these are token programs, and even where they are not, the numbers of citizens involved are not necessarily a benefit. Poorly managed volunteer programs can only lead to mistakes on a massive scale, rather than the positive impact originally intended.[7] The ways in which SERD/CHHDC residents could benefit from volunteer services were manifold. They ranged from shopping or presenting oneself to a potential employer to seeking legal services and day-care services for a dependent child. During FY 1974, SERD planned to inaugurate a volunteer program. Considering the volunteer programs that had failed (and many have done so in a dramatic fashion), the following activities and steps were seen as essential.

a. design and plan the program
b. recruit volunteers
c. select volunteers
d. train volunteers
e. supervise volunteers

The Volunteer Program would be implemented and supervised by the Chief of Programs.

Notes

1. Chamber of Commerce of the United States, *Marshaling Citizen Power to Modernize Corrections* (Washington, D.C.: Chamber of Commerce, 1972), p. 8.

2. National Parole Institute, *Uniform Parole Reports* (New York: National Council on Crime and Delinquency, November, 1972).

3. *Moving Toward Tomorrow: D.C. Department of Corrections, Summary Report 1967-72* (Washington, D.C.: D.C. Department of Corrections, undated), p. 44.

4. Data in this paragraph generally adapted from *Moving Toward Tomorrow: District of Columbia Department of Corrections, Summary Report 1967-72* (Washington, D.C.: D.C. Department of Corrections, undated), 66 pp.

5. The National Parole Institute, *Uniform Parole Reports* (New York: National Council on Crime and Delinquency, March, 1967 and February, 1973).

6. I.H. Scheier and J.L. Berry, *Guidelines and Standards for the Use of Volunteers in Correctional Programs* (Boulder, Colorado: National Information Center on Volunteers in Courts, August, 1972).

7. Ibid.

Appendixes

Appendix A:
Methodology Employed in the Case Study Evaluation

Introduction

This appendix describes the methods and techniques followed in collecting and analyzing the data for the evaluation and for the statistical computations contained in the case study presented in Chapter 5.

The information was collected by SERD and SERD/CHHDC staff members over a period of 12 months. Information and data contained for SERD/CHHDC have been verified and corrected, and reporting systems were refined during preparation of this case study (winter and spring, 1973).

The first step in the collection of information and data was to correct and verify existing data on SERD/CHHDC residents. This was a relatively simple task because when the program started, a data-collection system had been designed based almost entirely on the MIS. When this task was completed, it was necessary to collect and verify comparable data for the other two youth programs operated by the D.C. Department of Corrections. This task was most difficult, and, though SERD can guarantee the accuracy of data presented in the case study for SERD/CHHDC, the accuracy of data used for the other two programs could not be verified to the same degree. The essential problems were two: Data on resident movement were not always recorded, and second, where data were recorded, accuracy had not always been verified. Thus in some cases SERD had to rely on gross numbers—generally, those reported by program staff.

Various reports prepared by D.C. Department of Corrections departments, including Youth Services, the Job Development Unit, the Data Processing Unit, the Parole Board, and the Business Office were reviewed and analyzed. An examination was made of other existing reports and materials of a national scope, such as U.S. Parole Reports and LEAA and U.S. Bureau of Prisons reports.

This appendix contains the following information: a detailed statement of the methods and techniques employed in the collection and verification of the data on SERD/CHHDC residents; a detailed explanation of how data were collected, verified, and treated in each of the tables contained in the case study in Chapter 5; and a justification for cost information used in the case study.

**The Collection, Verification and
Presentation of Data for SERD/CHHDC**

In February, 1972, SERD/CHHDC implemented a Management Information System (MIS) for a three-month test period. This system was introduced to allow staff to track residents through the program, so that staff, SERD, and DCDC could be advised of valuable information on a daily basis, and to refine and ensure constant verification of records and data maintained in the program. At the end of three months, the MIS was revised, and staff were trained in the use of the new forms and procedures. From the time MIS records were initiated, SERD/CHHDC resident records improved measurably.

In December, 1972, SERD decided to consolidate all known statistical information gathered previously on all residents admitted to the Center—including those admitted prior to February, 1972 (when the MIS records began). It was also recognized that, despite considerable improvement in the various areas, errors were still being made by the reporting staff, and it was hoped that, in the course of this consolidation, complete correction of the records could be effected.

This initial review of all actions by residents at SERD/CHHDC covered the 18-month period of July 1, 1971, to December 31, 1972, and was constructed in three 6-month cohorts. Each cohort was developed by the identification of all people admitted to the Center during the specific time period of the cohort, e.g., Cohort A covered intakes for the period July 1-December 31, 1971. In the course of developing this listing of admissions, great care was taken to verify the exact date of admission and the ultimate disposition of each resident at the Center and to verify each incident ascribed to a given resident. To accomplish this, a total review of all SERD/CHHDC monthly escape, remand, and rearrest reports submitted to DCDC during this period was undertaken. In addition, the Center's monthly statistical reports to DCDC (which described the flow of residents in and out of the Center) were utilized to crosscheck the individual report numerical totals. Following this, the Center's Monthly Billing Record reports, which provided exact dates of in-count and out-count status and exact dates and specific dispositions of each of the residents during a given month, were thoroughly examined and crosschecked (by name) against the other information described here. All of this research was further checked and doublechecked by a review of the Center's daily action log and the Center's daily count figures reported to DCDC.

The cohorts were constructed chronologically, i.e., by date of admission to the Center. On completion of all of the foregoing, the information contained in the roster was then meticulously matched against each resident's file (and when necessary against his institutional jacket as well) to ensure complete and total accuracy of all information, including his date of admission to SERD/CHHDC, his DCDC number, the spelling of his name, his ultimate disposition, and the exact, official date of disposition.

This information was then developed into chronological rosters (by cohort) of all admissions to the Center. Once this was accomplished, it became relatively simple to determine for any given time period, the number of program failures and successes that had occurred. In January, 1973, of course, a similar roster was begun to cover all new admissions to the Center between January 1 and June 30, 1973 (Cohort D). In addition to the cohort rosters, SERD developed a simple card file for each person ever served by SERD/CHHDC on which the same information is recorded. This card file and the basic rosters were updated and audited monthly to insure that DCDC was receiving the most factual and accurate information possible.

All tables and other statistical information provided in this case study are based on the information contained in these meticulously researched rosters. For this reason, SERD has every confidence in the correctness of the information presented here, even though some of the information is at variance with that published in the Youth Services Annual Statistical Report for FY 1972, dated December, 1972.

The Presentation of Data in the Tables in this Report

Table 5-1: SERD/CHHDC and CTCY Population Data by Resident Man-days for Quarter Years—FY 1972 and 1973

Table 5-1 contains population data by resident man-days on a quarterly basis for FY 1972 and 1973. Data were available from the daily count records and other sources noted for SERD/CHHDC for FY 1972 and FY 1973. The numbers of man-days for June, 1973, for both SERD/CHHDC and CTCY were estimated. SERD/CHHDC daily figures were checked carefully and verified against the actual number of residents in the facility on each day reported during FY 1972. During FY 1973, the reporting procedures for maintaining daily count records had been refined and the procedure provided for the maintenance of a daily count card file that was audited monthly by the Chief of Operations. FY 1973 data were further verified by SERD staff before this information was reported.

FY 1973 data for CTCY were taken from the daily count sheets distributed by the DCDC Youth Services Division. Because records were not available for weekends, the number of man-days for in-count and out-count reported on Fridays were, in most cases, carried through the weekend. It should be pointed out that this procedure gives CTCY the benefit of a few extra days because in most cases, the daily count reported for both in-count and out-count on Mondays was lower than the Friday figure—indicating that incidents occurred on the weekends. When the information was received and tabulated for each month, the quarters were totaled and entered on the table. The total resident man-days was computed by adding the total in-count and total out-count man-days. The percentages were computed using the quarterly totals as a base.

In sum, SERD/CHHDC data in Table 5-1 are accurate. Two variables question

CTCY data. First, the data are only as accurate as daily count sheets are accurate, and from SERD/CHHDC experience, reporting errors are known to exist in daily count sheets. Second, no weekend data were available for CTCY. As a result of these two variables, in all probability, the estimates of man-days of service is probably high for CTCY.

Table 5-2: Population Movement:
Youth Services Community Correctional
Centers—FY 1972

The following list describes the items in Table 5-2.

1. *Paroles:* This refers to residents actually paroled during FY 1972 from each of the programs. Data for CTCY for this item are from the D.C. Parole Board. Data for SERD/CHHDC are from verified program records. Data for Youth Progress House are from the roster of residents served during FY 1972 which Youth Progress House prepared for the DCDC Division of Planning, Research, and Evaluation.
2. *In-program failures:* This includes escapes, arrests, and remands of residents in the program. The number for SERD/CHHDC was taken from carefully checked and verified program records. The number for Youth Progress House was taken from the FY 1972 roster of residents (noted previously) prepared for DCDC. The number of failures for CTCY was taken from the monthly reports prepared by CTCY and submitted to the DCDC Youth Services Division.
3. *Other actions:* "Other actions" represent people who were released from the community correctional centers other than arrests, remands, escapes, and paroles. This includes people completing parole, halfway-backs, deceased residents, etc. For SERD/CHHDC, this figure was taken from checked and verified program records. Data for Youth Progress House was taken from the roster of residents submitted to DCDC. These data were checked and no "other actions" were identified for YPH. For CTCY, data prepared during the first six months of FY 1972 for DCDC presented a roster of resident names and dispositions. This list was checked and three "other actions" were identified. On the monthly reports submitted to the Department of Corrections, CTCY did not report any "other actions" for the remainder of the year.
4. *In program at June 30, 1972:* This item represents the number of residents (total of in-count and out-count) still in the program on June 30, 1972, for which no disposition had been determined. The number for SERD/CHHDC was taken from checked and verified program records. The total for Youth Progress House was taken from the dates of program release listed on the

Youth Progress House roster of residents submitted to DCDC for FY 1972. The number for CTCY was taken from the daily count sheet information prepared for the Department of Corrections and reported to them by CTCY.

5. *Unaccounted for:* The "unaccounted for" cell represents the difference between the total residents reported served by CTCY during FY 1972 and the items previously noted and reported on this table. This indicates that during FY 1972, SERD was unable to trace 46 people through monthly reports of the D.C. Youth Services Division, the D.C. Parole Board, and other sources. Part of this discrepancy can be attributed to the discrepancies in the number of paroles reported by CTCY and checked and verified through the D.C. Parole Board and other sources. This information is described in the explanation for Table 5-4.

6. *Total residents:* This represents the numerical total of the numbers reported in each column and is the base for the percentages for each of the items within each program. For SERD/CHHDC, this represents the total number of residents served during FY 1972. For Youth Progress House, this represents the total number of residents served during FY 1972 as reported by Youth Progress House to DCDC. For CTCY, this represents the total residents served during FY 1972 as reported by CTCY to the D.C. Department of Corrections on monthly report summaries.

Table 5-3: Population Movement:
SERD/CHHDC and CTCY–FY 1973

Table 5-3 presents population movement for SERD/CHHDC and CTCY during FY 1973 (July 1, 1972, through June 30, 1973) and for the last six months of that year (January 1 through June 30, 1973)–the period when SERD's population was nearer capacity than at any other time during the study period. The description for each of the items and the basis for the source of the information for Table 5-3 is the same as that reported in Table 5-2. Data for Youth Progress House for FY 1973 were not available. The June, 1973, totals for both programs were estimated based upon average populations and results for each of the months during the fiscal year.

Table 5-4: Parole and
Recidivism Data

Parole and recidivism data for SERD/CHHDC and CTCY are presented for FY 1972 and 1973. For SERD/CHHDC, the number of paroles and the status of each person paroled in the program from its inception have been checked through the following sources: SERD/CHHDC records, individual resident files—both Center files and institutional files—the D.C. Parole Board, individual C&P officers for each resident paroled, DCDC Youth Services Division records, families of parolees, and actual contacts with people paroled.

Data presented for CTCY represent information supplied by the D.C. Parole Board. This number is different from that reported by CTCY to the DCDC Youth Services Division. Monthly reports that were reviewed at the Youth Services Division submitted by CTCY reported 134 paroles for FY 1972 and 118 paroles in FY 1973 (June, 1973, estimated). Beginning with this number, SERD went to the Parole Board to obtain a list of all CTCY parolees for the two fiscal years. The master records in the Parole Board produced lists of 124 names for FY 1972 and 96 names for FY 1973.[a] SERD carefully screened the list through the following sources: lists of residents supplied by all youth programs to DCDC, the computerized data file for each resident in the data-processing system at DCDC, the individual C&P Officers of residents, the present population at the D.C. Jail, the Youth Centers, and the Reformatory, and other records at Lorton, the D.C. Jail, and the DCDC Business Office. From these sources, the Parole Board lists were screened down to the following totals for CTCY parolees for FY 1972 and 1973: for FY 1972, 97, and for FY 1973, 86. The differences between the original Parole Board lists and the numbers included were the following. In some cases, a person escaped, was remanded, or arrested shortly before his parole became effective, and this had not been noted in the Parole Board records; however, the parole was not granted. In some cases, the parole hearing for residents was physically held at CTCY, and the Parole Board had credited the resident paroled as being a person residing at CTCY, while, in fact, the parolee was a resident at SERD/CHHDC, Shaw #3, or Youth Progress House. SERD staff also found some duplicate listings. These were eliminated through matching DCDC numbers and information contained in institutional files. From the list of names, SERD followed up with C&P Officers, the Department data-processing system, and other sources, including the Police Department, the Youth Centers, and the D.C. Jail, to determine the present status of the people on the two lists. This search produced the following.

For residents paroled during FY 1972:
    Paroles revoked: 29
    Still on parole: 62
    Status unknown or not able to trace: 6
    Total: 97
For residents paroled during FY 1973:
    Paroles revoked: 18
    Still on parole: 63

---

[a]Possibly, part of the reason for the discrepancy between CTCY figures and Parole Board figures was that CTCY reported halfway-backs as paroles. For purposes of this evaluation, halfway-backs were classified as "other actions."

Status unknown or not able to trace: 5
Total: 86

The final screening of all records on parole recidivism was completed in June, 1973; these data are accurate through June 25, 1973. In Table 5-4, the percent of recidivism for CTCY is based upon the total parolees reported by the Parole Board excluding those whose status is unknown.[b] If one assumes that all of those 11 whose status is unknown are successes, the CTCY recidivism rate would be 25.7 percent for the two years, or 29.9 percent in FY 1972 and 20.9 percent in FY 1973.

Table 5-5: Time on Parole for SERD/CHHDC Parolees as of June 26, 1973

The length of time on parole for all residents paroled from SERD/CHHDC during the two fiscal years (the entire time of operation of the Center at this writing) were checked through the Department of Corrections' records, data-processing systems, the Youth Services institutions, the D.C. Jail, Lorton, and through personal contacts with C&P Officers, families of parolees, and parolees themselves. Once SERD determined those residents who had been returned to an institution, it was possible to determine the length of time these residents had been on the street from their date of parole. The cut-off date for this table was determined to be June 26, 1973, or such time as an action occurred that returned the resident to an institution.

Table 5-6: Comparison of SERD/CHHDC and CTCY Costs per Successful Parolee—FY 1973

The section on the Comparative Cost Data in this case study discusses cost per successful parolee data contained on Table 5-6. As pointed out previously, the status of five parolees from CTCY for FY 1973 could not be traced; therefore, these were excluded from the computations. (If these five were all considered successful parolees and included, CTCY's cost per successful parolee would be reduced to $6,380, a reduction of approximately $500.) The number of parolees was derived as noted in the preceding section. The costs used for this table are explained in the following section.

---

[b]Before this table was prepared, the procedures followed and the discrepancies were discussed by telephone with the D.C. Department of Corrections' Division of Planning, Research, and Evaluation. They supported SERD's contention that these discrepancies were due partly to inaccurate reporting techniques and concurred that Parole Board data should be the most reliable source.

*Table 5-7: Comparisons of
SERD/CHHDC and CTCY Costs
per Man-day—FY 1973*

Costs data presented on Tables 5-6 and 5-7 for SERD/CHHDC came from monthly invoices and verified costs submitted to the Department of Corrections. Costs for June, 1973, for SERD/CHHDC were estimated.

CTCY cost information was derived from the following sources. The FY 1973 costs for CTCY were estimated on the basis of information provided in the proposed Department of Corrections Budget for FY 1974. The adjusted base operating budget for youth community centers in FY 1973 was reported as $699,900. This amount covered both SERD/CHHDC and CTCY. The subtraction of the projected SERD/CHHDC costs of $385,316 for FY 1973 left a balance of $314,584 available for CTCY. This amount was assumed to reasonably represent CTCY's direct operating costs for FY 1973.

To determine total costs (direct costs plus department overhead) for CTCY in FY 1973, an estimate of overhead costs was derived on the basis of information contained in the Department of Corrections' budget. This was done by first totaling all funds in the budget that could be identified as overhead administrative, and support costs. The total of about $7,880,000 in overhead costs was then divided by the estimated total number of man-days of service provided by the Department—about 1,414,000. This computation resulted in an estimate of $5.57 as the average overhead cost per man-day for the Department of Corrections in FY 1973.

The average overhead cost per man-day of $5.57 was assumed to apply to CTCY as well as the Department of Corrections as a whole. The total overhead cost for CTCY in FY 1973 was computed by multiplying $5.57 by 21,413 (the number of man-days of service calculated for CTCY in FY 1973). On this basis, overhead costs for CTCY were estimated as $119,270. By adding this amount to the estimated direct costs for CTCY, a total cost figure of $433,854 was derived for FY 1973.

CTCY's direct costs for FY 1971 through 1973 were computed on a reported and estimated basis to show the year-to-year changes in major cost components and also to compare reported costs with a more comprehensive estimate of direct costs. The difference between reported direct costs and estimated direct costs is that reported costs apparently did not include all fringe benefit costs, such as unemployment compensation, workmen's compensation, and a portion of employee's health and life insurance. The reported cost of fringe benefits for CTCY in FY 1971 was equal to 7.4 percent of basic payroll. The government retirement contribution is 7.0 percent of payroll, which would leave only 0.4 percent for all the other legally required fringe benefit items. The average cost to the federal government for these items is 2.8 percent of payroll. Therefore, an additional 2.4 percent of payroll was added to the 7.4 percent reported to derive total fringe benefit costs. In addition to the difference in fringe benefit costs, the estimated costs for CTCY also include a GS-9 Job Development Specialist who is assigned to CTCY but is charged to another budget category.[c]

The increase in CTCY's estimated personnel costs was slightly over 10 percent in both 1972 and 1973. However, the increases in nonpersonnel direct costs were 28.4 percent in FY 1972 and only 10.8 percent in FY 1973.

The sharp increase in nonpersonnel costs in FY 1972 may indicate that there was incomplete accounting for nonpersonnel costs in 1971, which may have been corrected in 1972, or there may be some other explanation for the increase.

It is interesting to note that the estimated increase of 10.1 percent in total direct costs in FY 1973 is identical to the increase in personnel costs. This would seem to lend some support to the estimate of total direct costs because the personnel cost data are quite solid, and personnel costs account for over 60 percent of total costs.

---

[c]The Annual Report FY 1972 (dated August 7, 1972), of the Job Development Unit of the D.C. Department of Corrections reported that in FY 1972 this unit reported 1,399 cases served who were residents of halfway houses. Of these, 903 (63.5 percent) were CTCY residents.

Appendix B: Glossary of Terms

C&P Refers to Classification and Parole Officers or the Classification and Parole Department at DCDC which supervises all parolees upon parole from any DCDC institution or community center.

CAP Credit Advancement Program, a behavior-modification program that was the treatment program adopted at SERD/CHHDC.

CTCY The Community Treatment Center for Youth located at 1825-13th Street, N.W., in Washington, D.C.; a community treatment facility for youthful offenders operated by the D.C. Department of Corrections.

DCDC Acronym used for the District of Columbia Department of Corrections.

Escape (1) A resident who has left a Center unauthorized by his counselor or other staff member; (2) a resident who has failed to return to the Center two hours past curfew time.

Fiscal Year 1972 This is the period beginning July 1, 1971, and ending June 30, 1972.

Fiscal Year 1973 The period beginning July 1, 1972, and ending June 30, 1973.

Halfway-back A person on parole who is assigned by his parole officer to a community treatment center for a short period of time, usually for disciplinary purposes.

LEAA The Law Enforcement Assistance Administration of the U.S. Department of Justice which supports research, planning, and program operations in the criminal justice field.

In-count A resident of a community correctional center who resides in the facility.

Man-days This refers to the number of days in a given time period (quarter-years in Table 5-1) multiplied by the number of residents served in that period. The estimate of total possible man-days of service SERD/CHHDC could provide was based on 365 days in a year.

MIS A Management Information System that contained all records and reports on activities of SERD/CHHDC and tracked resident movement through the program.

Out-count A resident of a community correctional center who is living in the community but who is still under the custody of center staff.

Parolee Throughout this report "parolees" refer to residents of community treatment centers who have been released on parole. Halfway-backs were not included in this group.

Parole failure rate Throughout this report the parole failure rate is the proportion of people on parole who had been returned to an institution based on the total number of paroles for that period.

Rearrest A resident who had been rearrested by the police department, FBI, or other police jurisdiction.

Recidivism Return to an institution of a person who had previously been confined. This includes people who may have been paroled from a community treatment center but were sent to another institution on detainer.

Remands A community center resident who was returned to the institution, D.C. Jail, or to the custody of the Department of Corrections.

SERD Acronym used for Social, Educational Research and Development, Inc., a human development research and development firm.

SERD/CHHDC The SERD/Congress Heights Human Development Center, a community treatment center for youthful offenders located at 406 Condon Terrace, S.E., in Washington, D.C., operated by Social, Educational Research and Development, Inc., under contract to the D.C. Department of Corrections.

Urine Surveillance Program A program whereby urine samples are laboratory-tested to determine use of heroin and methadone.

YPH Youth Progress House, a therapeutic community program operated by the D.C. Department of Corrections serving youthful offenders from time of sentence through completion of parole. This program previously was called the Youth Crime Control Project (YCCP) and is located at 1719-13th Street, N.W., in Washington, D.C.

Youth Center References throughout this report to Youth Center(s) refer to Youth Center #1 and Youth Center #2 at the Lorton Complex in Lorton, Virginia. These are the minimum security institutions operated by the D.C. Department of Corrections for offenders convicted under the Federal Youth Corrections Act.

Bibliography

Bibliography

ABT Associates. *Design For An Evaluation of the Pre-Trial Intervention Program of the Manpower Administration, U.S. Department of Labor, Volumes I and II.* Cambridge, Massachusetts: ABT Associates, 1971.

Accountability: Technical Group Report No. 1. Helena: Montana Commission on Post-Secondary Education, May, 1974.

Ackoff, Russel L. *The Design of Social Research.* Chicago: The University of Chicago Press, 1953.

A Comparative Study of the Community Parole Center Program, Research Report No. 63. Sacramento: California Youth Authority, 1973.

Acquiland, J.N. "Monroe County Probation Program: A Follow-Up Report." *Probation and Parole* 4 (Summer, 1972):55-62.

Adams, Stuart. *Evaluative Research in Corrections: A Practical Guide.* Washington: Government Printing Office, March, 1975.

_____. "Evaluative Research in Corrections: Status and Prospects." *Federal Probation* 38 (March, 1974):14-21.

Albright, Ellen, et al. *Evaluation In Criminal Justice Programs: Guidelines and Examples.* Washington: Government Printing Office, June, 1973.

Aledort, Stuart L. and Morgan Jones. "Euclid House: A Therapeutic Community Halfway House For Prisoners." *American Journal of Psychiatry* 130 (March, 1973):186-239.

Alexander, Merle E. *Residential Center: Corrections In The Community.* Washington: U.S. Bureau of Prisons, 1970.

American City Corporation. *Making Evaluation Research Useful.* Columbia, Maryland: The Urban Life Center, 1971.

American Correctional Association. *Manual of Correctional Standards.* College Park, Maryland: American Correctional Association, 1966.

American Institutes for Research. *Evaluative Research: Strategies and Methods.* Pittsburgh, Pennsylvania: American Institutes for Research, 1970.

An Analysis of Recidivism Among Men Released From MCI Concord During 1966. Boston: Massachusetts Department of Correction, 1972.

An Analysis of Recidivism Among Men Released From MCI Norfolk During 1966. Boston: Massachusetts Department of Correction, 1972.

An Analysis of Recidivism Among Men Released From MCI Walpole During 1966. Boston: Massachusetts Department of Correction, 1972.

A Time To Act. Washington: Joint Commission on Correctional Manpower and Training, undated.

Atkinson, John W. "Motivational Determinants of Risk-Taking Behavior." *Psychological Review* 64 (1957):359-372.

Azzi, C.F. and J.C. Cox. "Equity and Efficiency in Evaluation of Public Programs." *Quarterly Journal of Economics* 87 (August, 1973):495-502.

Babst, Dean V. and Carl D. Chambers. "New Dimensions For Parole Expectancy Research." *Criminology* 10 (1972):353-365.

Bennett, L.A., D.E. Sorenson and H. Forshay. "The Application of Self-esteem Measures in a Correctional Setting: I. Reliability of the Scale and Relationship To Other Measures." *Journal of Research in Crime and Delinquency* 8 (January, 1971):1-9.

Benson, Margaret. "A Whole-hearted Look at Half-way Houses." *Canadian Journal of Corrections*, July, 1967.

Berecochea, John E. and George E. Sing. *The Effectiveness of a Halfway House for Civilly Committed Narcotic Addicts, Research Report No. 42.* Sacramento: California Department of Corrections, Research Division, August, 1971.

Blumstein, Alfred. *A National Program of Research, Development, Test, and Evaluation of Law Enforcement and Criminal Justice.* Arlington, Virginia: Institute for Defense Analyses, 1968.

Bolin, David C. and Laurence Kivens. "Evaluation in a Community Mental Health Center: Huntsville, Alabama." *Evaluation* 2 (1974):26-35.

Boone, John O. *A Study of Community-based Correctional Needs in Massachusetts.* Boston: Massachusetts Department of Correction, 1972.

Brandstatter, A.F. and A.A. Hyman. *Fundamentals of Law Enforcement.* Beverly Hills, California: Glencoe Press, 1971.

Brewer, Donald D. *Correctional Personnel, A Plan for Action.* Springfield, Virginia: National Technical Information Service, 1968.

Burr, E. "A Five-Year Study of 112 Women Parolees of New York State Hospitals." *Psychiatric Quarterly Supplement* 20 (1946):73-85.

California Youth Authority. *California: Standards For Juvenile Homes, Ranches, and Camps, Probation Series N23.* Sacramento: California Youth Authority, 1972.

California Youth Authority. *Follow-up of Wards Discharged from CYA During 1965, Research Report No. 64.* Sacramento: California Youth Authority, 1973.

Carrier, N.A. "The Relationship of Certain Personality Measures to Examine Performance Under Stress." *Journal of Educational Psychology* 48 (1957):510-520.

Committee on Government Operations, Research and Technical Programs Subcommittee. *The Use of Social Research in Federal Domestic Programs*, Parts I, II, III, and IV. Washington, D.C.: Government Printing Office, 1967.

Comptroller General of the United States. *Report to Congress: Need for Improving the Administration of Study and Evaluation Contracts.* Washington, D.C.: General Accounting Office, 1971.

Correctional Officer Training in Behavior Modification, An Interim Report. Washington, D.C.: Rehabilitation Research Foundation, 1972.

Cowden, J.E. and L. Monson. "Analysis of Some Relationships Between

Personality Adjustment, Placement, and Post-Release Adjustment of Delinquent Boys." *Journal of Research in Crime and Delinquency* 6 (January, 1969):63-70.

Criminology and Corrections Programs. Washington, D.C.: Joint Commission on Correctional Manpower and Training, July, 1968.

Davis, George. "A Study of Adult Probation Violation Rates by Means of the Cohort Approach." *The Journal of Criminal Law and Criminology and Police Science*, March, 1964.

Development Associates, Inc. *Handbook For The Evaluation of Career Education Programs.* Washington, D.C.: Bureau of Occupational and Adult Education, U.S. Office of Education, August, 1974.

Dick, W. and N. Hagerty. *Topics In Measurement: Reliability and Validity.* New York: McGraw-Hill Book Company, 1971.

Diggory, J.C. *Self-Evaluation: Concepts and Studies.* New York: John Wiley and Sons, Inc., 1966.

Doherty, Victor W. and Walter E. Hathaway. "Goals and Objectives in Planning and Evaluation: A Second Generation." *NCME Measurement in Education* 4 (Fall, 1972):1-8.

Dorfman, Robert, ed. *Measuring Benefits of Government Investments.* Washington, D.C.: The Brookings Institution, 1965.

Drucker, Peter F. *Management: Tasks, Responsibilities, Practices.* New York: Harper & Row, Publishers, 1973.

DuMars, R.C. *Counselor Training for Correctional Officers—An Experiment in Lay Counselor Training.* Ann Arbor: University Microfilms, 1969.

Eash, Maurice J. et al. *Evaluation Designs for Practitioners. TM Report No. 35.* Washington, D.C.: National Institutes of Education, D/HEW, December, 1974.

Ekstein, Daniel G. "Improving Counselor Effectiveness by Means of Feedback and Encouragement." Paper presented at the annual meeting of the American Psychological Association, 82nd, New Orleans, Louisiana, August, 1974.

Empey, LaMar T. *Peer Group Influences in Correctional Programs.* Submitted to the President's Commission on Law Enforcement and Administration of Justice, Washington, D.C., 1967.

Empey, LaMar T. and M.L. Erickson. *Provo Experiment: Evaluating Community Control of Delinquency.* Lexington, Massachusetts: Lexington Books, D.C. Heath and Company, 1972.

Empey, LaMar T. and S.G. Lubeck. *Silverlake Experiment: Testing Delinquency Theory and Community Intervention.* Chicago: Aldine Publishing Company, 1971.

Erickson, Rosemary J. et al. *Paroled But Not Free.* New York: Behavioral Publications, 1973.

Festinger, Leon and Harold H. Kelley. *Changing Attitudes Through Social Contact.* Ann Arbor: University of Michigan, Institute for Social Research, 1951.

Florida Division of Youth Services. *Study of Florida's Halfway Houses: Their Benefits, Costs, and Effectiveness—Part I.* Tallahassee: Florida Division of Youth Services, undated.

Force, R.C. *The Air Force's New Correctional Treatment Team.* Amarillo, Texas: 3320th Retraining Group, Amarillo Air Force Base, 1961.

French, Elizabeth G. "Some Characteristics of Achievement Motivation." *Journal of Experimental Psychology* 50 (1955):232-236.

French, Elizabeth G. and F.H. Thomas. "The Relationship of Achievement Motivation to Problem Solving." *Journal of Abnormal Social Psychology* 56 (1958):45-48.

Frye, R.L. "The Effect of Orientation and Feedback of Success and Effectiveness on the Attractiveness and Esteem of the Group." *Journal of Social Psychology* 70 (1966):205-211.

Glaser, Daniel. "From Revenge to Resocialization: Changing Perspectives in Combating Crime." *The American Scholar* 40 (1956):15.

_____. "Problems in the Evaluation of Treatment Programs." *Rehabilitating the Narcotic Addict.* Washington, D.C.: Government Printing Office, 1967.

Glaser, Edward M. and Thomas E. Backer. "A Clinical Approach to Program Evaluation." *Evaluation* 1 (1972):50-59.

Grant, Frank A. *An Experimental Approach To Adult Offenders.* Huntsville, Texas: Sam Houston State University, 1972.

Guttentag, Marcia. "Subjectivity and its use in Evaluation Research." *Evaluation* 1 (1973):60-65.

Hagood, Margaret Jarman and Daniel O. Price. *Statistics For Sociologists.* New York: Henry Holt and Company, 1952.

Hecht, Judith A. *Effects of Halfway Houses on Neighborhood Crime Rates and Property Values: A Preliminary Survey.* Washington, D.C.: Department of Corrections, 1970.

Holder, H.D. and D.S. Alberts. *Taking Corrections into the Community: An Evaluation Design.* Raleigh: Institute of Human Ecology and North Carolina Department of Corrections, 1971.

Holland, W.E. and H.H. Huntoon. "Evaluation of Experimental Social Service Delivery Systems at the Community Level: An Organizational Effectiveness View." *Community Mental Health Journal* 10 (Spring, 1974):41-51.

Hoshino, G. "Social Services: The Problem of Accountability." *Social Service Review* 47 (Spring, 1973):373-383.

Houlihan, Kevin A. *Parole Outcome Studies: Adult Community Centers and Juvenile Halfway Houses.* Springfield: Illinois Department of Corrections, 1971.

Hudson, C.H. *An Experimental Study of the Differential Effects of Parole Supervision for a Group of Adolescent Boys and Girls, Summary Report.* Washington, D.C.: Government Printing Office, March, 1973.

Institute of Criminal Justice and Criminology. *Reintegration of the Offender into the Community.* College Park: University of Maryland, 1972.

Interdepartmental Council to Coordinate all Federal Juvenile Delinquency Programs. *An Analysis of Federal Juvenile Delinquency and Related Youth Development Programs for Juvenile Delinquency Planners.* Washington, D.C.: Government Printing Office, February, 1973.

International Halfway House Association. *Guidelines and Standards for Halfway Houses and Community Treatment Centers.* Washington, D.C.: Government Printing Office, 1973.

Iwanicki, Edward F. *Activity Analysis: An Approach to Improving the Evaluation Design of Ongoing Educational Programs.* Paper presented at the Annual Meeting of the National Council on Measurement in Education, Chicago, Illinois, April, 1974.

James, Howard. *Children in Trouble: A National Scandal.* Boston: The Christian Science Publishing Society, 1969.

James, Ralph E. and Lawrence M. Miller. *Rehabilitation by Behavior Management: A Training Manual and Staff Achievement Program for Correctional Agency Personnel.* Raleigh, North Carolina: Human Behavior Institute, Inc., 1972.

Jenkins, O.W. et al. *A Longitudinal Follow-up Investigation of the Post-release Behavior of Paroled or Released Offenders.* Elmore, Alabama: Experimental Manpower Laboratory for Corrections, Draper Correctional Center, 1973.

Kaplan, Howard B. and Joseph H. Meyerwitz. "Evaluation of a Halfway House: Integrated Community Approach in the Rehabilitation of Narcotic Addicts." *International Journal of the Addictions* 4 (1970):292-304.

Kaufman, Roger A. "A Systems Approach to Accountability in Education." Paper prepared for Bureau of Elementary and Secondary Education, U.S. Office of Education, Washington, D.C., January 25, 1971.

Keller, Oliver J., Jr. and Benedict S. Alper. *Halfway Houses: Community-centered Correction and Treatment.* Lexington, Massachusettts: Lexington Books, D.C. Heath and Company, 1970.

Kennedy, Robert F. "Halfway Houses Pay Off." *Crime and Delinquency* 10 (1964):1-7.

Kerlinger, Fred N. *Foundations of Behavioral Research.* New York: Holt, Rinehart and Winston, Inc., 1973.

King, L.W. et al. "Accountability, Like Charity, Begins at Home." *Evaluation* 2 (1974):75-77.

Kirby, B.C. "Crofton House: An Experiment with a County Halfway House." *Federal Probation* 33 (March, 1969):53-58.

_____. *Crofton House Final Report.* San Diego: San Diego State College, 1970.

Klapmuts, Nora. "Community Alternatives to Prison." *Crime and Delinquency Literature* 5 (June, 1973):305-337.

Koontz, Harold and Cyril O'Donnell. *Principles of Management: An Analysis of Managerial Functions.* New York: McGraw-Hill Book Company, 1972.

Lazarsfeld, Paul F., William H. Sewell, and Harold L. Wilensky. *The Uses of Sociology.* New York: Basic Books, Inc., 1967.

Lazzaro, Victor, ed. *Systems and Procedures: A Handbook for Business and Industry,* 2d ed. Englewood Cliffs, New Jersey: Prentice-Hall, Inc., 1968.

Lebowitz, Harriet M. "Work Release Prediction Tables" from *Federal Work Release Evaluation, Fiscal Year 1967.* Washington, D.C.: U.S. Bureau of Prisons, February, 1972.

Levitan, Sar A. *Federal Social Dollar in its own Back Yard.* Washington, D.C.: Bureau of National Affairs, 1973.

Littlefield, C.L., M. Rachel Frank, and Donald L. Caruth. *Office and Administrative Management: Systems Analysis, Data Processing, and Office Services,* 3rd ed. Englewood Cliffs, New Jersey: Prentice-Hall, Inc., 1970.

Los Angeles (County) Probation Department. *Comparative Analysis of the Willowbrook-Harbor Intensive Services Program, March 1, 1965, Through February 28, 1966. Research Report No. 28.* Los Angeles: Probation Department, 1966.

McCollum, John W. "The Uses of a Management Information System in a Community-based Treatment Center for Offenders." Paper presented to the 1972 Annual Meeting of The American Society of Criminology, November 19-26, 1972, in Caracas, Venezuela.

McFarlane, Fred R. "Behavioral Assessment: A Vital Tool for the Inmate's Rehabilitation." *Georgia Journal of Corrections* 1 (1972):142-147.

Management and Behavioral Science Center et al. *Planning and Designing for Juvenile Justice.* Washington, D.C.: Law Enforcement Administration, U.S. Department of Justice, August, 1972.

Marshall, Kaplan, Gans, and Kahn. *An Evaluation of "Newgate" and Other Prisoner Education Programs: Research Design.* San Francisco: Marshall, Kaplan, Gans, and Kahn, March 1972.

Martinson, R.M. *Treatment Ideology and Correctional Bureaucracy—A Study of Organizational Change.* Ann Arbor, Michigan: University Microfilms, 1968.

Minnesota Department of Corrections. *Follow-up Study of 166 Juveniles who were Released from State Group Homes from July 1, 1969, Through June 30, 1972.* St. Paul: State of Minnesota, 1973.

Moberg, David O. and Richard C. Ericson. "A New Recidivism Outcome Index." *Federal Probation* 36 (June, 1972):50-57.

Moyer, Fred D., Edith E. Flynn, Fred A. Powers, and Michael J. Plautz. *Guidelines for the Planning and Design of Regional and Community Correctional Centers For Adults.* Urbana: Department of Architecture, University of Illinois, 1970.

Mullen, Edward J., James R. Dumpson, et al. *Evaluation of Social Intervention.* San Francisco: Jossey-Bass, Inc., Publishers, 1972.

Myren, Richard A. "Decentralization and Citizen Participation in Criminal Justice Systems." *Public Administration Review* 32 (October, 1972): 718-738.

National Advisory Commission on Criminal Justice Standards and Goals.

Corrections—Report of the National Advisory Commission on Criminal Justice Standards and Goals. Washington, D.C.: Government Printing Office, 1973.

National Advisory Commission on Criminal Justice Standards and Goals. *Community Crime Prevention.* Washington, D.C.: Government Printing Office, 1973.

National Institute of Law Enforcement and Criminal Justice. *Community-based Corrections in Des Moines: A Coordinated Approach to the Handling of Adult Offenders.* Washington, D.C.: Law Enforcement Assistance Administration, U.S. Department of Justice, undated.

National Institute of Mental Health. *Community Based Correctional Program Models and Practices.* Washington, D.C.: Government Printing Office, 1971.

National Institute of Mental Health. *Community-Based Treatment Programs for Narcotic Addiction.* Washington, D.C.: Government Printing Office, 1968.

National Institute of Mental Health. *Diversion from the Criminal Justice System.* Washington, D.C.: Government Printing Office, 1972.

New Approaches to Diversion and Treatment of Juvenile Offenders. Criminal Justice Monograph of papers on topics presented at the Fourth National Symposium on Law Enforcement Science and Technology, May 1-3, 1972, conducted by The Institute of Criminal Justice and Criminology, University of Maryland. Washington, D.C.: Law Enforcement Assistance Administration, U.S. Department of Justice, June, 1973.

Newman, Charles L. "Educational Issues and Strategies for the Field of Corrections." *The Quarterly* 24 (Spring, 1967):56-60.

Nicholson, Richard C. "Use of Prediction in Caseload Management." *Federal Probation* 32 (1968):54-58.

Norman, Sherwood. *Juvenile Detention and Community Responsibility.* Institute Proceedings, Social Work Institutes, Department of Sociology and Social Work, Texas Women's University, Denton, Texas, October 8, 1968.

_____. *Standards for the Detention of Children and Youth.* New York: National Probation and Parole Association, 1957.

Palmer, T. and A. Herrera. *Community Treatment Project Post-Discharge Analysis: An Updating of the 1969 Analysis for Sacramento and Stockton Males.* Sacramento: California Youth Authority, 1972.

_____. *CTP's San Francisco Experiment (1965-69): Post-Discharge Behavior of Differential Treatment and Guided Group Interaction Subjects.* Sacramento: California Youth Authority, 1972.

Parole Corrections Project. *The Mutual Agreement Program, Resource Document No. 3.* College Park, Maryland: American Correctional Association, November, 1973.

Perspectives on Correctional Manpower and Training. College Park, Maryland: American Correctional Association, 1970.

Pettibone, John M. "Community-Based Programs, Catching up with Yesterday and Planning for Tomorrow." *Federal Probation* 37 (September, 1973):3-8.

Pioneer Cooperative Affiliation. *Statistical Report for the Chance Program, Jan.-Dec. 1971.* Seattle: Pioneer Cooperative Affiliation, 1972.

Pleck, J.H. and S.I. Simon. *Effectiveness of a Correctional Halfway House.* Washington, D.C.: National Institute of Law Enforcement and Criminal Justice, 1969.

Powers, Edwin. "Half-Way Houses: An Historical Perspective." *American Journal of Correction* 21 (July-August, 1959):20-22.

Prentice-Hall Editorial Staff. *Handbook of Successful Operating Systems and Procedures with Forms.* Englewood Cliffs, New Jersey: Prentice-Hall, Inc., 1964.

"Prison Halfway Houses Meet Rising Opposition." *The New York Times,* November 26, 1971.

Reed, James A. "Program Evaluation Research." *Federal Probation* 38 (March, 1974):37-42.

Richmond, M.S. "Correctional Programming in the Community." *Criminologica* 6 (1968):2-9.

Richmond, Samuel B. *Operations Research for Management Decisions.* New York: The Ronald Press Company, 1968.

Rivlin, Alice M. *Systematic Thinking For Social Action.* Washington, D.C.: Brookings Institution, 1971.

Rossi, Peter H. and Walter Williams, eds. *Evaluating Social Programs: Theory, Practice, and Politics.* New York: Seminar Press, 1972.

Rudoff, Alvin and T.C. Esselstyn. "Evaluating Work Furlough: A Follow-up." *Federal Probation* 37 (1973):48-53.

Rudoff, Alvin, T.C. Esselstyn, and G.L. Kirkham. "Evaluating Work Furlough." *Federal Probation* 35 (March, 1971):34-38.

Scheier, I.H. and J.L. Berry. *Guidelines and Standards For The Use of Volunteers in Correctional Programs.* Boulder, Colorado: National Information Center on Volunteers in Courts, August, 1972.

Scott, E.M. and K.L. Scott. *Criminal Rehabilitation—Within and Without Walls.* Springfield, Illinois: Charles C. Thomas, Publisher, 1973.

Shields, M. "Evaluation Model For Service Programs." *Nursing Outlook* 22 (July, 1974):448-451.

Showalter, R. and R. Dart. *Career Ladders in a Criminal Justice System—An Exploratory Study.* Bethesda, Maryland: Social Development Corporation, 1973.

Sigurdson, Herbert R., A.W. McEachern, and Robert M. Carter. "Administrative Innovations in Probation Service: A Design for Increasing Effectiveness." *Crime and Delinquency* 19 (July, 1973):353-366.

Smith, Robert L. *A Quiet Revolution: Probation Subsidy.* Washington, D.C.: Government Printing Office, 1971.

_____. "California's Probation Subsidy—History and Policy Issues." Probation Research Conference Speech: University of California, Davis, March 25-26, 1970.

Smith, Robert R., Lynda A. Hart, and Michael A. Milan. *Correctional Officer Training in Behavior Modification: An Interim Report.* Washington, D.C.: Manpower Administration, U.S. Department of Labor, May, 1971.

Social, Educational Research and Development, Inc. *A Model Social Service Program for a County Jail.* New York: Praeger Publishers, 1972.

_____. *A Model Social Service Program for the Montgomery County Detention Center.* Silver Spring, Maryland: SERD, Inc., February 12, 1971.

_____. *A Survey and a Plan of Action for Education and Training Services in the Maryland Correctional Training Center in Hagerstown, Maryland.* Silver Spring, Maryland: SERD, Inc., October 15, 1969.

_____. *Draft of a Proposed Management Systems and Procedures Design for Youth Service Bureaus in Illinois, Volume II.* Chicago: SERD, Inc., April 11, 1975.

_____. *Standards for the Design, Development, and Operation of Community Correctional Centers in the State of Maryland.* Chevy Chase, Maryland: SERD, Inc., June 15, 1973.

_____. *The SERD/Congress Heights Human Development Center (SERD/ CHHDC): A Review of Program Results: 1971-1973.* Washington, D.C.: SERD, Inc., June 1973.

South Carolina Department of Corrections. *Community Pre-Release Programs, Annual Report, 1970-71.* Columbia: South Carolina Department of Corrections, 1971.

Southeastern Correctional and Criminological Research Center. *Community Contact and Inmate Attitudes: An Experimental Assessment of Work Release.* Tallahassee: Florida State University, 1973.

Special Report on Adult Offenders in the Community Residential Treatment Program. Washington, D.C.: Bureau of Rehabilitation of the National Capital Area, 1972.

Stanford Research Institute. *A Benefit/Cost Model to Evaluate Educational Programs.* Menlo Park, California: Stanford Research Institute, January, 1968.

Strategies for Meeting Occupational Training and Manpower Needs—Four Developmental Projects. Springfield, Virginia: National Technology Information Service, 1968.

Sullivan, Howard J. and Robert W. O'Hare, eds. *Accountability in Pupil Personnel Services: A Process Guide for the Development of Objectives, Monograph Number 3.* Fullerton, California: California Personnel and Guidance Association, 1971.

Tappan, Paul W. *Comparative Survey of Juvenile Delinquency, Part I, North America.* New York: Department of Economic and Social Affairs, United Nations, 1958.

Targets For In-Service Training. Washington, D.C.: Joint Commission on Correctional Manpower, 1967.

Training for Corrections—Rationale and Techniques. Carbondale: Southern Illinois University, 1968.

Trice, Harrison M. and Paul M. Roman. "Evaluation of Training: Strategy, Tactics and Problems." *Training Information Sources, No. 3.* Madison, Wisconsin: American Society for Training and Development, August, 1973.

Tropman, John E. and Karl H. Gohlke. "Cost/Benefit Analysis: Toward Comprehensive Planning in the Criminal Justice System." *Crime and Delinquency* 19 (July, 1973):315-322.

Turner, Merfyn. "The Lessons of Norman House." *Annals of the American Academy of Political and Social Science* 381 (1969):39-46.

U.S. Department of Health, Education, and Welfare. *Annual Report of Federal Activities in Youth Development, Juvenile Delinquency and Related Fields: Fiscal Year 1971.* Washington, D.C.: Government Printing Office, 1972.

Venezia, P.S. *Pre-Trial Release to Supportive Services of High Risk Defendants: The Second-Year Evaluation of the Des Moines Community Corrections Project.* Davis, California: NCCD Research Center, 1972.

Waldo, Gordon P., Theodore G. Chiricos, and Leonard E. Dobrin. "Community Contact and Inmate Attitudes: An Experimental Assessment of Work Release." *Criminology* 11 (November, 1973):345-381.

Wilkins, Leslie T. and Don M. Gottfredson. *Research, Demonstration and Social Action.* Washington, D.C.: The Office of Juvenile Delinquency and Youth Development, U.S. Department of Health, Education, and Welfare, 1969.

Willett, Lynn H. "A Model for Assessing Impact of Institutional Studies." Paper presented at the Annual Meeting of North Central States AERA/SIG for Community/Junior College Research, Iowa City, Iowa, July, 1974.

Wolman, Benjamin B., ed. *Dictionary of Behavioral Science.* New York: Van Nostrand and Reinhold Company, 1973.

Zimiles, Herbert. "A Radical and Regressive Solution to the Problem of Evaluation." Paper presented at the Meeting of the Minnesota Round Table in Early Childhood Education, Wayzata, Minnesota, June, 1973.

Index

Activities, SERD/CHHDC, 7, 70, 90
Admissions, SERD/CHHDC, 73
Advanced Rehabilitation Phase, CAP Phase IV, SERD/CHHDC, 6
Anacostia, 69
Average Monthly Population
  CTCY, 75
  SERD/CHHDC, 73

Behavioral Technology Consultants, Inc., 8
Bibliography, 109
Bonus System, SERD/CHHDC, 6

CAP
  Advanced Rehabilitation Phase, Phase IV, 6
  Defined, 107
  Early Rehabilitation Phase, Phase II, 6
  Evaluation of, 85
  Intermediate Rehabilitation Phase, Phase III, 6
  Orientation, Phase I, 6
  Out-Count, Phase V, 7
  Phases Described, 6
  Staff Training for, 8, 91
Case Study, 69
Center for Group Studies, 8
Certificate of Occupancy, 73
Chief of Operations, SERD/CHHDC, 4, 5
Chief of Programs, SERD/CHHDC, 4, 5
Coed Facilities, Suggested, 90
Cohort Analysis, 88, 98
Community Center for Youth. See CTCY
Community Correctional Centers
  Case Study—one center, 69
  Description of, xiv, 1, 2
  Evaluation of, 12
  Forms and Formats for, 23
  Information System for, 51
  Procedures for, 23
  Purposes of, 72
Community Policy Committee, SERD/CHHDC, 7
Comparative Analyses of SERD/CHHDC and CTCY, 69
Computation of
  Fringe Benefits, CTCY, 104
  Overhead, CTCY, 104
Cost
  Comparisons, 81
  Computation of, 103
  Evaluation of, 16
  Incarceration, of, 72
  Per In-Count Man-Day, CTCY, 82, 83

Per In-Count Man-Day, SERD/CHHDC, 82, 83
Per Man-Day, CTCY, 72, 82, 83
Per Man-Day, SERD/CHHDC, 71, 81, 82, 83
Per Successful Parole, CTCY, 81, 82
Per Successful Parole, SERD/CHHDC, 81, 82
Total, CTCY, 81, 82
Total, SERD/CHHDC, 81, 82, 83
Cost per In-Count Man-Day
  CTCY, 82, 83
  SERD/CHHDC, 82, 83
Cost per Man-Day
  CTCY, 72, 82, 83
  SERD/CHHDC, 71, 82, 83
Costs, Total
  CTCY, 81, 82
  SERD/CHHDC, 81, 82
Costs of Evaluation, 16
Costs per Successful Parolee
  CTCY, 81, 82
  SERD/CHHDC, 81, 82
Credit Advancement Program. See CAP
CTCY
  Average Monthly Population, 75
  Comparative Analyses, 70, 73
  Cost per Man-Day, 82, 83
  Cost per Successful Parole, 81, 82
  Cost, Total, 81, 82
  Costs, Computation of, 104
  Failure Rate, 71, 75, 77
  Fringe Benefits, Computation of, 104
  In-Program Failures, 75
  Location of, 70, 107
  Man-Days of Service, 73, 74
  Overhead, Computation of, 104
  Parolees, 71, 75, 76, 77
  Parole Revocations, 102
  Parole Successes, 77, 102
  Population Movement, 73, 74, 75, 101
  Recidivism Rate, 71, 102
  Successful Residents, 71, 75, 76

Daily Count Reports, 99, 100, 101
Data Analysis, 17, 18, 19, 97
Data Base
  Defined, 51
  How to Develop, 23, 51
Data Collection, 17, 23, 51
DCDC
  Automatic Data Processing Unit, 97
  Classification and Parole (C & P), 102, 103, 107

121

DCDC *(continued)*
  Community Center Goals, 4
  D.C. Jail, 61, 102, 103
  Defined, 107
  Division of Planning, Research, and Evaluation, 100, 103
  Job Development Unit, 97, 105
  Lorton Complex, 61, 103
  Urine Surveillance Program, 58, 71, 80
  Youth Centers, 3, 102, 108
  Youth Services Division, 70, 97, 99, 101, 102, 103
Department of Corrections, D.C. *See* DCDC
District of Columbia, Department of Corrections. *See* DCDC
Drug Abuse, 6, 57, 59, 60
Duty Officer System, SERD/CHHDC, 24, 71, 89

Early Rehabilitation Phase, CAP Phase II, SERD/CHHDC, 6
Earnings of Residents, SERD/CHHDC, 78
Employment of Residents, SERD/CHHDC, 78, 87, 91
Escape, 100, 107
Evaluation
  Bibliography on, 111
  Cohort Analysis, 88, 98
  Comparative Analysis, 14, 18, 69, 97
  Costs of, 14, 16
  CTCY, of, 69
  Data Base for, 23, 51
  Defined, 1, 2
  Expectations of, 19
  External, 14, 15
  Information System for, 51
  Internal, 14
  Issues, 21
  Limitations of, 11, 21
  Methodology, 17
  Planning for, 12
  Procedures and Steps in, 17
  Purposes of, 2
  Role of, 2
  Sample Case Study, 69
  SERD/CHHDC, of, 69
  Techniques, 11, 84
  Third-Party, 14
  Types of, 12, 14
Expectations of Evaluation, 19
Experimental Efforts, Suggested, 89
External Evaluation, 14, 15

Failure Rate
  CTCY, 71, 75, 76, 77
  Defined, 100, 101
  SERD/CHHDC, 71, 75, 76, 77, 78

Failures, Profile of SERD/CHHDC, 77, 84
Federal City College, 9
Federal Youth Corrections Act, 108
Felons, 3
Follow-Up
  Forms, 38
  Procedures, 23
Forms
  Family Information, 34, 35
  Follow-Up, 38
  Intake, 25
  MIS, 51
  Notification of Parole Date, 38, 45, 46
  Parole Progress Report, 38, 47, 89
  Plan, 37, 40
  Resident Agreement, 41, 57
  Sample Formats, 23, 51
  Summary, MIS, 62
Foster Care, 89
Fringe Benefits, Computation of CTCY, 104

George Washington University, The, 9
Glossary of Terms, 107
Goals
  DCDC Community Centers, 3, 4
  Evaluation, 19
  SERD/CHHDC, 4, 69, 70

Halfway Back, xiii, 100, 102, 107
Halfway House, xiii
Halfway In, xiii
Heroin, 59, 80
Howard University, 9

Identification of Objectives, 3, 14
Incentives
  Resident, 6, 87, 90
  Staff, 90
In-Count, 99, 107
Information System, 51
Inner Voices of Lorton, 8
In-Program Failures
  CTCY, 75, 76, 100
  SERD/CHHDC, 75, 76, 100
  YPH, 75
In-Program Successes. *See* Paroles
Intake
  Forms, 26, 28, 29, 30, 35
  Procedures, 25
Intensive Care Residents, SERD/CHHDC, 52, 58
Intermediate Rehabilitation Phase, CAP Phase III, SERD/CHHDC, 6
Internal Evaluation, 14
Interviewing, 17
Introduction, 1
Issues in Evaluating Community Correctional Centers, 21

Job Development, 78, 87, 89, 91
Johns Hopkins University, The, 9
Joint Efforts, Suggested, 89

Law Enforcement Assistance
  Administration. *See* LEAA
LEAA, 97, 107
Licensing, 89
Lorton, 3, 61, 102, 103
Lorton Complex, 3, 103, 108

Mail Surveys, 17
Management-by-Objectives Approach, 90, 91
Management Information System
  Defined, 51, 107
  Forms, 63
  How To Make Entries, 52
  Objectives of the MIS, 51, 84
  Procedures, 51, 84
  Reporting Codes, 53
  Resident Assessment Scale, 62
  Summary Forms, 62, 65
  Use of, 49, 51, 84, 88
  What Entries to Make, 54
  When To Make Entries, 53
  Where To Make Entries, 52
Man-Days of Service
  CTCY, 73, 74
  Defined, 107
  SERD/CHHDC, 73, 74
Methodology of Evaluation, 17
Methods and Procedures, Case Study, 96
MIS. *See* Management Information System
MIS FORMS, 63
Multiple Failures
  Recommendation for, 89
  SERD/CHHDC, 77

New Approaches, Suggested, 23, 51, 89, 90
New Programs, SERD/CHHDC, 90

Observations, 17
Operations Division, SERD/CHHDC, 4, 5, 90
Organizational Structure, SERD/CHHDC, 4, 5, 90
Orientation, CAP Phase I, SERD/CHHDC, 6
Out-Count
  Defined, 7, 73, 107
  CAP Phase V, SERD/CHHDC, 7
Overhead, Computation of CTCY, 104

Parole Board, D.C., 92, 97, 100, 102
Parole Revocations
  CTCY, 77, 102
  SERD/CHHDC, 77

Paroles
  Cost Per Parolee, 81, 82
  CTCY, 75, 76, 81, 82, 103
  Forms, 38, 44
  Length of Time on Parole, 71, 78, 103
  SERD/CHHDC, 75, 76, 81, 82
  Parolee, Defined, 107
  Procedures, 38
  Revocation of Parole, 77, 102
  Successful, 75, 77, 102
  YPH, 75
Parole Successes
  CTCY, 77, 101
  SERD/CHHDC, 77, 101, 103
Parole Supervision, Proposed, 91
Performance-Based Programs, Suggested, 90
Plans, SERD/CHHDC, 90
Policy and Procedures Manual
  Basis or need for, 23
  Content of, 24
  Development of, 23
  Distribution of, 23
  Organization of, 24
  Outline, suggested, 24
  Use of, 8, 23, 88
Policy Committee. *See* Community Policy Committee
Policy Statement, SERD/CHHDC, 4
Population Movement
  CTCY, 73, 74, 75, 76
  SERD/CHHDC, 72, 73, 74, 75, 76
  YPH, 75
Procedures
  Evaluation, 11, 17
  Follow-Up, 38
  Intake, 25
  Manual, 23
  Parole, 38
Procedures Manual, SERD/CHHDC, 8, 88
Program Plan, 37
Program Results, 71, 74, 75, 76, 77, 78, 79, 80, 81, 82, 83
Program Services Division, SERD/CHHDC, 4, 5, 90
Prompt, Defined, 90
Psychiatric Institute Foundation, 8
Purposes of Evaluation, 2

Reader's Guide, 9
Recidivism
  Defined, 108
  Rates of, 71, 77, 78, 101
Recidivism Rate
  CTCY, 71, 77, 101
  SERD/CHHDC, 71, 77, 78, 101, 103
Remand, Defined, 108
Research, Defined, 1, 2

Resident Incentives, 7, 90
Role of Evaluation, 2

Sample Case Study, 69
SERD, 1, 51, 80, 81, 89, 91, 92, 97, 98, 101, 102, 103, 108
SERD/CHHDC
  Activities, 7, 88
  Admissions, 73
  Average Monthly Population, 73
  Bonus System, 6, 91
  CAP, 6, 71, 88, 91
  Chief of Operations, 4, 5
  Chief of Programs, 4, 5
  Community Policy Committee, 7
  Comparative Analyses, 71
  Cost per Man-Day, 71, 81, 82, 83
  Cost per Successful Parole, 81, 82
  Cost, Total, 81, 82, 83
  Credit Advancement Program, 6, 7, 71
  Defined, 108
  Duty Officer System, 71, 89
  Earnings of Residents, 78
  Employment of Residents, 78
  Evaluation of, 69
  Failure Rate, 71, 75, 76, 77, 78
  Failures, Profile of, 77, 84
  Goals, 6, 69, 70
  Incentives, 6, 7, 90
  In-Program Failures, 75, 76, 100
  Intensive Care, Residents in, 52, 58
  Job Development, 78, 87, 89, 91
  Location of, 3, 69, 108
  Management by Objectives, 90
  Man-Days of Service, 73, 74, 99
  Multiple Failures, 77, 89
  New Programs, 7, 90
  Operations Division, 4, 5
  Organizational Structure of, 4, 5
  Parole, Length of Time on, 78, 103
  Parole Revocations, 77, 78, 101, 103
  Paroles, Number of, 71, 75, 76, 77, 78, 100, 101
  Parole Successes, 71, 77, 78, 101, 103
  Parole Supervision, Proposed, 91
  Plans, 90
  Policy Committee, 7
  Policy and Procedures Manual, 8, 71, 78
  Policy Statement, 4
  Population Movement, 72, 73, 74
  Program Services Division, 4, 5
  Recidivism Rate, 71, 77, 78, 101, 103
  Subsistence Paid, 79
  Successful Residents, 71, 75, 76, 77, 78, 100, 101, 103
  Successful Residents, Profile of, 84
  Table of Organization, 5
  Training Programs, 8, 91
  Treatment Approach, 6, 71, 88
  Urine Surveillance, 55, 80
  Volunteers, 92
SERD/Congress Heights Human Development Center. *See* SERD/CHHDC
Social, Educational Research and Development, Inc. *See* SERD
Southeast Washington, D.C. *See* Anacostia
Staff Incentives, 90
Subsistence Collections, SERD/CHHDC, 79
Successful Residents, Profile of SERD/CHHDC, 84
Success Rate
  CTCY, 71, 75, 76, 77
  Paroles, 71, 75, 76, 77, 78, 100, 101
  SERD/CHHDC, 71, 75, 76, 77, 78

Table of Organization, SERD/CHHDC, 5
Third Party Evaluation, 13, 14, 69
Training Programs, SERD/CHHDC, 8, 91
Treatment Approach, SERD/CHHDC, 6, 71, 88

Urine Surveillance Program
  DCDC, 7, 71, 80
  SERD/CHHDC, 7, 58, 71, 80

Validity Checks, 18, 97
Volunteers, 92

YCCP. *See* YPH
Youth Centers, 3, 108
Youth Crime Control Project. *See* YPH
Youth Offenders, 3, 69, 70
Youth Progress House. *See* YPH
Youth Services Division. *See* DCDC
YPH
  Comparative Analyses, 73, 75, 100
  Defined, 108
  In-Program Failures, 75, 100
  Location of, 73, 108
  Paroles, 75, 100
  Population Movement, 75, 101

Zoning, SERD/CHHDC, 89

About the Authors

Social, Educational Research and Development, Inc. (SERD) is a social science, educational research, and human development corporation specializing in social and educational research, training, development, and consulting services. The firm, founded in 1964, serves private industry, public and private agencies, schools and colleges, libraries, hospitals, prisons, and community groups in the areas of education; training; social, psychological, and economic research; evaluation; minority-group relations; and community development.

Mercedese M. Miller has been a SERD staff member since 1967 and has been Vice President for Administration and Planning since 1969. She is responsible for overall project management; designing, developing, and applying internal evaluation and management tools and techniques; and for contract and staff management and supervision. She has developed, implemented, and evaluated information systems, policy and procedures manuals, fiscal and cost analyses procedures, personnel procedures manuals, and staff and consultant training manuals.

SERD has completed a number of projects in the correctional field including interview studies of former convicts, evaluation and design of educational programs for prisoners, operation of a halfway house for former youth offenders in Washington, D.C., evaluations of institutional and community correctional programs, evaluations of diversion and juvenile programs, design and development of management procedures, manuals, and information systems for institutions and community programs, recidivism studies, and cost-benefit analyses.

The firm has home offices in Washington, D.C. and branch offices in Chicago, Illinois, Honolulu, Hawaii and St. Thomas, the U.S. Virgin Islands.